THE BATTLE OF GETTYSBURG

Decisive Events in American History

THE

BATTLE OF GETTYSBURG

1863

BY

S A M U E L   A D A M S   D R A K E

AUTHOR   OF   "BURGOYNE'S   INVASION,"   "TAKING   OF
LOUISBURG," ETC.

"The world will little note, nor long remember, what we say here"
ABRAHAM LINCOLN

BOSTON
L E E   A N D   S H E P A R D   P U B L I S H E R S
1 0 MILK STREET
1892

PRESS OF
ROCKWELL AND CHURCHILL
BOSTON

THE BATTLE OF GETTYSBURG 1863

By Samuel Adams Drake
Originally Published in 1892 by Lee and Shepard Publishers

©2001 DSI digital reproduction
First DSI Printing: January 2001

Published by **DIGITAL SCANNING, INC.**
Scituate, MA 02066
www.digitalscanning.com

Trade Paperback ISBN: 1-58218-326-0
Hardcover ISBN: 1-58218-327-9
eBook ISBN: 1-58218-325-2

Digital Scanning and Publishing is a leader in the electronic republication of historical books and documents. We publish our titles as eBooks, as well as traditional hardcover and trade paper editions. DSI is committed to bringing many traditional and little known books back to life, retaining the look and feel of the original work.

CONTENTS.

―――――

THE BATTLE OF GETTYSBURG

1863

I

GETTYSBURG[1]

STRIPPED of the glamour which has made its every stick and stone an object of eager curiosity or pious veneration, Gettysburg becomes a very plain, matter-of-fact Pennsylvania town, of no particular antiquity, with a very decided

The Town.

Dutch flavor in the names and on the tongues of its citizens, where no great man has ever flourished, or anything had happened to cause its own name to be noised abroad, until one day in the eventful year 1863—the battle year—fame was suddenly thrust upon it, as one might say, not for a day, but for all time. The dead who sleep in the National Cemetery[2] here, or who lie in unknown graves about the fields and woods, and counting many times more than the living, help us to understand how much greater was the battle of Gettysburg than the town which has given it its name.

Gettysburg is the market town—or borough, accurately speaking—of an exclusively farming population, planted in one of the most productive sections of the Keystone State. It is the seat of justice of the county. It has a seminary and college of the German Lutheran Church, which give a certain tone and cast to its social life. In short, Gettysburg seems in all things so entirely devoted to the pursuits of peace, there is so little that is suggestive of war and bloodshed, even if time had not mostly effaced all traces of that gigantic struggle,[3] that, coming as we do with one absorbing idea in mind, we find it hard to reconcile the facts of history with the facts as we find them.

There is another side to Gettysburg—a picturesque, a captivating side. One looks around upon the landscape with simple admiration. One's highest praise comes from the feeling of quiet satisfaction with which the harmony of nature reveals the harmony of God.

The Landscape.

You are among the subsiding swells that the South Mountain has sent rippling off to the east. So completely is the village hid away among these green swells that neither spire nor steeple is seen until, upon turning one of the numerous low ridges by which the face of the country is so cut up, you enter a valley, not deep, but well defined by two opposite ranges of heights, and Gettysburg lies gleaming in the declining sun before you—a picture to be long remembered.

Its situation is charming. Here and there a bald ridge or wooded hill, the name of which you do not yet know, is pushed or bristles up above the undulating prairie-land, but there is not one really harsh feature in the landscape. In full view off to the northwest, but softened by the gauzy haze of a midsummer's afternoon, the towering bulk of the South Mountain, vanguard of the serried chain behind it, looms imposingly up between Gettysburg and the Cumberland Valley, still beyond, in the west, as landmark for all the country round, as well as for the great battle-field now spreading out its long leagues before you; a monument more aged than the Pyramids, which Napoleon, a supremely imaginative and magnetic man himself, sought to invest with a human quality in the minds of his veterans, when he said to them, "Soldiers! from the summits of yonder Pyramids forty ages behold you." In short, the whole scene is one of such quiet pastoral beauty, the village itself with its circlet of fields and farms so free from every hint of strife and carnage, that again and again we ask ourselves if it can be true that one of the greatest conflicts of modern times was lost and won here.

Yet this, and this alone, is what has caused Gettysburg, the obscure country village, to be inscribed on the same scroll with Blenheim, and Waterloo, and Saratoga, as a decisive factor in the history of the nations. Great deeds have lifted it to monumental proportions. As Abraham Lincoln so beautifully said when dedicating the National Cemetery here, "The brave men, living and dead, who struggled here have consecrated it far above our power to add or detract. The world will little note, nor long remember, what we say here, but it can never forget what they did here."

Those noble words ought to be the guiding inspiration of every one who intends adding his own
feeble impressions of this great battle to what has
been said before.

The strategic importance that Gettysburg sud-
Strategic   denly assumed during Lee's invasion of
Importance.   Pennsylvania, in July, 1863, first demands a little of our attention. Yet it seems certain that neither Meade nor Lee had thought of
it as a possible battle-ground until accident thrust
it upon them. At his first setting out on this
campaign Lee had not been able to say, with the
map before him, "I will fight a battle either in
this or that place," because he had marched not
toward, but away from, his adversary, and, so far
as can be known, without choosing beforehand a
position where Meade would have to come and
attack him. For his part, so long as Meade was
only following Lee about, the Union general cannot be said to have had much voice in the matter.
It was Lee who was really directing Meade's
march. True enough, Meade did select a battlefield, but not here, at Gettysburg; nor do we
know, nor would it be useful to inquire, whether

Lee could have been induced to fight just where
Meade wanted him to. As Lee fought at Gettysburg only because he was struck, it is probably
beyond any man's power to say that if this had
not happened, as it did, Lee would have marched
on toward Baltimore, knowing that Meade's army
lay intrenched in his path. There is a
homely maxim running to the effect
that you can lead a horse to water,
but cannot make him drink. The two generals,
therefore, merely launched their columns out hit
or miss, like men playing at blind-man's-buff.

Playing at Blind-Man's-Buff.

Gettysburg lies at the apex of a triangle of
which Harrisburg and Baltimore form the base
angles, at north and south—Harrisburg being
only thirty-six and Baltimore about fifty miles
distant. York and Carlisle also lie either on
or so near this triangle as to come within its
scope as a basis for military operations. Placed
at Gettysburg, an army threatened all of these
points.

From a military point of view there are but two
features about Gettysburg on which the eye would
long rest. These are the two ridges, with a broad

valley between, heaved up at east and west and

Topographical running off south of the town. They
Features. stand about a mile apart, though the

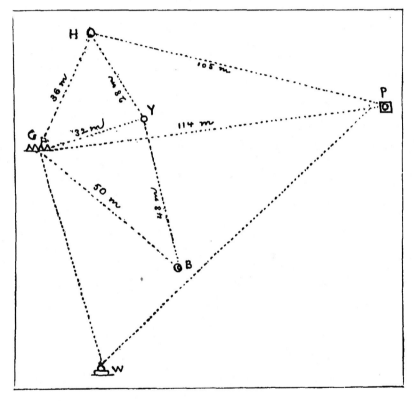

Diagram showing strategic value of Gettysburg. H., Harrisburg;
G., Gettysburg; P., Philadelphia; Y., York; B., Baltimore; W., Washington.

distance is sometimes less than that. As it nears
Gettysburg the easternmost ridge glides down, by

a gentle slope, into what may be called a plain, in comparison with the upheavals around it, although it is by no means a dead level. Yet it is open because the ridges themselves have stopped short here, forming headlands, so to speak, above the lower swells. On coming down off this ridge the descent is seen to be quite easy—in fact, two roads ascend it by so gradual a rise that the notion of its being either high or steep is quite lost, and you are ready to discard off-hand any preconceived notion about its being a natural stronghold. It is mostly on this slope that Gettysburg is built, its houses extending well up toward the brow, and its cemetery occupying the brow itself. Hence, although the centre of Gettysburg may be three-fourths of a mile from the cemetery gate, the town site is in fact but a lower swell of the historic ridge which has since taken the name of its graveyard— Cemetery Ridge.

Across this valley, again, the western ridge, which looks highest from the town, has what Cemetery Hill has not, namely, a thin fringe of

Baltimore and Taneytown Roads.

Cemetery Hill.

trees skirting its entire crest, thus effectually masking the view in that direction; and it is further distinguished by the cupola of the Lu-
Seminary Ridge. theran Seminary,[4] seen rising above trees at a point opposite the town, and giving its name to this ridge—Seminary Ridge. Both ranges of heights are quite level at the top, and easily traversed; so also the slopes of both are everywhere easy of ascent, the ground between undulating, but nowhere, except far down the valley, badly cut up by ravines or watercourses. Indeed, better ground for a fair stand-up fight it would be hard to find; for all between the two ridges is so clear and open that neither army could stir out toward its opponent without being detected at once—the extreme southern part of the valley excepted. In this respect I take the liberty of observing that the actual state of things proved very different from that conveyed in some of the published accounts, wherein Cemetery Ridge is represented as a sort of Gibraltar.

A very brief survey, however, suggests that an army could be perfectly hid behind the trees of

Seminary Ridge, as well as better sheltered from artillery fire, while one stretched out along the bare and treeless summit of Cemetery Ridge would be without such screen or protection.

The description must be a little farther pursued, if the battle is to be at all intelligently followed.

Enough for the two main ridges enclosing Gettysburg and its valley. We come now to that most striking feature of the landscape, notably on the side of Cemetery Ridge, but more or less characteristic of both sides of the valley. This is the group of hills standing off from Cemetery Ridge at either end, just as if, at some remote time, this ridge had formed a continuous chain, the summits of which had been cleanly shaved off at the centre, leaving these isolated clusters to show where the wasting forces had passed. From different points of view we may see one or both of them rising above the ridge like giant watch-towers set at the extremities of some high embattled wall.

Let us first take the northernmost cluster, formed of Wolf's, McAllister's, and Culp's hills.

It is seen to be thrown back behind
Culp's Hill. Cemetery Hill, to which Culp's Hill
alone is slenderly attached by a low ridge, so
making an elbow with it, or, in the military phrase,
a refused line. Between Culp's Hill and Wolf's
Hill flows Rock Creek, the shallow stream so
often mentioned in connection with the battle, its
course lying through a shaggy ravine.[5] The
ravine and stream of Rock Creek
Rock Creek. threw Wolf's Hill somewhat out of
the true line of defence, but the merest novice in
military art sees at a glance why the possession of
Culp's Hill was all-essential to the security of
Cemetery Hill, since there is little use in shutting
the front door if the back door is to be left
standing open.

The same is just as true of the southernmost
group, composed of Little and Great Round Tops,
two exceedingly picturesque summits, standing up
above the generally monotonous contours about
them in strong relief. They also were wooded
The Round from base to summit, and they show,
Tops. even more distinctly than the first
group, where the crushing out or denuding forces

have been at work, in shelves or crevices of broken ledge at the highest points, in ugly bowlders crop-
The Devil's   ping out on the slopes, in miry gullies
Den.   crawling at their feet, but most of all in the deformed heap of ripped-up ledges, topped with coppices and scattered trees, thrust out from Little Round Top and known as the Devil's Den.[6]

When it is added that the way is open between the two Round Tops to the rear of Cemetery Ridge, the importance of holding them firmly becomes self-evident; and inasmuch as the greatest natural strength of this ridge lay at its extremities, or flanks, *so its weakness would result from a neglect to occupy those flanks.*

This line was assailable at one other point. As it approaches Little Round Top the ridge sinks away to the general level around it, or so as to
The Swale.   break its continuity, thus. leaving a gap
              more or less inviting the approach of an enemy. The whole extent of this crooked line, at which we have just glanced, is about two and a half miles.

Down below, in the valley, there is another swell of ground, hardly worth dignifying by the name of ridge, yet assuming a certain importance, nevertheless, first because it starts from the town close under Cemetery Hill,

Emmettsburg Road.

thence crossing the valley diagonally till it becomes merged in Seminary Ridge, at a point nearly opposite to the Round Tops, and next because the Emmettsburg road runs on it. In brief, its relation to the battle was this: it ran from the Union right into the Confederate right, so traversing the entire front of both armies. It had an important part to play in the second day's battle, as we shall soon see, for, though occupying three days, Gettysburg was but a series of combats in which neither army employed its whole force at any one time.

[1] Gettysburg is the county seat of Adams County; is one hundred and fourteen miles west of Philadelphia. Pennsylvania College is located here.

[2] The National Cemetery was dedicated by Abraham Lincoln, Nov. 19, 1863; it is a place of great and growing interest and beauty. The National Monument standing on this ground, where sleeps an army, was dedicated by General Meade in 1869. The monument itself was designed by J. G. Batterson, of Hartford, Conn., the statuary by Randolph Rogers. In 1872 the cemetery was transferred to the national government. A large part of the adjoining ridge is in charge of the Gettysburg Battlefield Memorial Association, a corporation formed under the laws of Pennsylvania for the preservation of the field

and its landmarks. No other battle-ground was ever so distinctly marked or so easily traced as this.

[3] Shells remain sticking in the walls of some buildings yet. A memorial stone at the steps in front of the Lutheran church, on Chambersburg street, indicates the spot where Chaplain Howell, of the 90th Pennsylvania Volunteers, was shot dead while entering the church, then being used as a hospital.

[4] The Lutheran Seminary was used both as a hospital and observatory by the Confederates. Lee's headquarters were in a little stone house quite near the seminary buildings, which are not more than half a mile from the centre of Gettysburg.

[5] In 1863 all these hills were much more densely wooded than now, so forming an impenetrable screen to their defenders.

[6] The bowlder-strewn strip of ground lying between Devil's Den and Little Round Top is the most impressive part of the field, I think.

II

THE MARCH INTO PENNSYLVANIA

IT is in no way essential to relate in detail how
Lee's army, slipping away from ours on the
Rappahannock,[1] and after brushing out of its
Lee in   path our troops posted in the Shen-
Maryland.   andoah Valley, had been crossing the
Potomac into Maryland since the 21st of June,
by way of the Cumberland Valley, without firing
a shot.[2]

A very unusual thing in war it is to see an
army which has just been acting strictly on the
His Bold   defensive suddenly elude its adversary
Strategy.   for the purpose of carrying the war
into that enemy's country! It marks a new
epoch in the history of that war, and it supposes
wholly altered conditions. In this particular instance Lee's moves were so bold as almost to
savor of contempt.

It is enough to know that Lee was now in

Pennsylvania, at the head of seventy thousand men, before our army reached the Potomac in pursuit of him, if following at a respectful distance be called a pursuit.

At no period of the war, their own officers said, had the Confederates been so well equipped, so well clothed, so eager for a fight, or so confident of success; and we may add our own conclusions, that never before had this army taken the field so strong in numbers, or with such a powerful artillery.[3]

State of his Army.

The infantry were armed with Enfield rifles, fresh from British workshops, and it is probable that no equal number of men ever knew how to use them better. Indeed, we consider it indisputable that the Confederates greatly excelled the Union soldiers as marksmen. Most of them were accustomed to the use of firearms from boyhood; in some sections they were noted for their skill with the rifle. The Confederates, therefore, were nearly always good shots before they went into the army, while the Union soldiers mostly had to acquire what skill they could after going into the ranks. In the

Superiority as Marksmen.

South the habit of carrying arms was almost universal: in the North it was not only unusual, but unpopular as well as unlawful.

Man for man, the Confederate cavalry was also superior to the Union horse, because in one sec-

Superiority in Cavalry.
tion riding is a custom, in the other a pastime rarely indulged in. Consequently, it took months to teach a Union cavalryman how to ride,—a costly experiment when your adversary is already prepared,—whereas if there is anything a Southerner piques himself upon, it is his horsemanship.

Lee's cavalry had preceded the infantry by nearly a week, reaching Chambersburg on the

Cavalry Advance.
16th, seizing horses and provisions for the use of the army behind them, and spreading consternation to the gates of Harrisburg itself. Having loaded themselves with plunder unopposed, they then fell back upon the main army, thus leaving it in some doubt whether

Cumberland Valley raided.
this raid had accomplished all it designed, or was only the prelude to something for which it was serving as a mask.[5]

All doubts were set at rest, however, when, on the 23d, Ewell's dust-begrimed infantry came tramping into Chambersburg, regiment after regiment, hour after hour, until the streets fairly swarmed Ewell at Chambersburg. with them. Though the houses were shut up, a few citizens were in the streets, or looking out of their windows at the passing show, as men might at the gathering of a storm-cloud about to burst with destructive fury upon them; and though the time was hardly one for merriment, we are assured that some of these lookers-on could not refrain from "pointing and laughing at Hood's ragged Jacks" as they marched along to the tune of "Dixie's Land." "This division," remarks the partial narrator, "well known for its fighting qualities, is composed of Hood's Soldiers. Texans, Alabamians, and Arkansians, and they certainly are a queer lot to look at. They carry less than any other troops; many of them have only got an old piece of carpet or rug as baggage; many have discarded their shoes in the mud; all are ragged and dirty, but full of good-humor and confidence in themselves and their general.[6] They answered the numerous taunts of the Chambersburg ladies with cheers and laughter." To the scowling citizens the Confederates would call out from the ranks, "Well, Yank, how far to Harrisburg? How far to Baltimore? What's the charge at the Continental?" or some such innocuous bits of irony as came into heads turned, no doubt, at the thought of standing unchallenged on Northern soil, where nothing but themselves recalled war or its terrors, or at sight of the many evidences of comfort and thrift to which they themselves were strangers. But we shall meet these exultant ragamuffins ere long under far different circumstances.

This was Lee's corps of observation, destined to do most of the hard marching and fighting which usually falls to the lot of the cavalry, as it was mostly composed of old, well-seasoned soldiers, who had been accustomed, under the lead of Jackson, to win their victories largely with their legs. Part marched through the town, and went into camp on the Carlisle road, part occupied the pike leading toward Gettysburg; sentries were posted in the streets, a military commandant was appointed, and for the time being Chambersburg fell wholly under rebel rule, which, so long as it remained the army headquarters, we are bound to say does not appear to have been more onerous than circumstances would warrant.

Ewell's corps was followed, at one day's march, by the main body, comprising Hill's and Long- Main Army street's corps, with whom marched Lee comes up. himself, the man on whom all eyes, North and South, were now turned.

As soon as the main body had come up Ewell moved straight on toward Carlisle and Harrisburg Ewell to with two divisions, while his third turned Carlisle. off to the east, toward York, with the view of drawing attention away from the main object by seeming to threaten Baltimore or Phila- Early to delphia.[7] It was to strike the Susque- York. hanna at Columbia, and get possession of the railway bridge there, as a means of passing over to the north side of that river to Harrisburg.

This division (Early's) passed through Gettys- burg on the 26th,[8] reaching York the next day. On the 28th his advance arrived at the Susque- Early at hanna too late to save the railway bridge Gettysburg. from the flames.[9] On this same day

Ewell's advance encamped within four miles of Harrisburg, where some skirmishing took place.

Here, then, was Lee firmly installed within striking distance of the capital of the great Keystone State, and by no means at so great a distance Region seized from Philadelphia or Washington as by Lee. not to make his presence felt in both cities at once.

If he had not come prepared to fight every soldier that the Federal government could bring against him—to fight even against odds—what was he doing here in the heart of Pennsylvania?

The army which followed Lee into Pennsylvania was brave and devoted—none more so. It looked up to him with a species of adoration, born of an abiding faith in his genius. Reasoning from experience, the belief that Spirit of his it would continue to beat the Union Army. army was not unfounded. At any rate, it was universal. Thus led, and imbued with such a spirit, no wonder the Confederate army considered itself invincible.

Thus followed, Lee, or Uncle Robert, as he was familiarly called by his soldiers, though no man could be more aristocratic in his tastes or manners, was accustomed to exact greater efforts from them, both in marching and fighting, than the Union generals ordinarily could from their better-fed, better-clothed, and better-disciplined troops.

A pen portrait of General Lee himself, as he appeared at this time, seems necessary to the historical completeness of this sketch. It is drawn by a British colonel, [10] on leave with Lee's army, where he found himself quite at home. He says:

Lee's Portrait. "General Lee is, almost without exception, the handsomest man of his age I ever saw. He is fifty-six years old, tall, broad-shouldered, very well made, well set up—a thorough soldier in appearance; and his manners are courteous and full of dignity. He generally wears a well-worn long gray jacket, a high black felt hat, and blue trousers tucked into his Wellington boots. I never saw him carry arms, and the only marks of military rank are the three stars on his collar. He rides a handsome horse which is extremely well groomed. He himself is very neat in his dress and person, and in the most arduous marches, as after the retreat from Gettysburg, when everybody else looked and was extremely dirty, he always looked smart and clean."

In an order commending the behavior of his

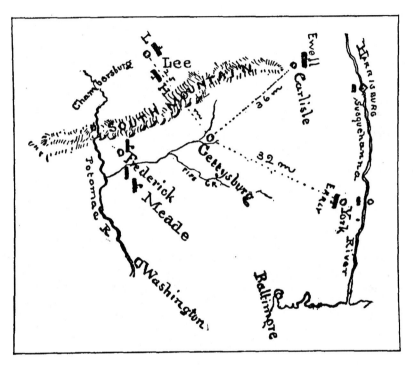

Positions, June 28th.

men while on the march, Lee called attention to certain excesses which he declared his intention of repressing in a summary manner.

The region to which the Confederate operations were now confined is indicated by the accompany-

ing map. It will be seen that Lee had not hesitated to scatter his army considerably.

Leaving Ewell before Harrisburg, Early at
York, and Lee himself at Chambersburg, we will
look first at the state of feeling brought about
by this daring invasion, which had been urged
from Richmond on the theory that *the road to
peace lay through Pennsylvania, via Washington.*

[1] He withdrew two corps, by his left, to Culpepper, leaving one in
the trenches of Fredericksburg. Had this corps been crushed while
thus isolated, as it ought, Lee's invasion must have ended then and
there.

[2] A glance at the map shows how the northerly bend of the Potomac
facilitated an invasion by this route. The outposts at Harper's Ferry
and Winchester having been forced, there was nothing to stop the
enemy's advance.

[3] The Confederate army comprised three infantry corps, and one of
cavalry. Each corps had three divisions, each division averaged a little
over four brigades, of which there were thirty-seven present at Gettysburg. The British Colonel Freemantle, who accompanied Lee's army,
puts the strength of these brigades at two thousand eight hundred men
each. The relative strength of the army corps was more nearly equal
than in those of the Union army. The Confederates brought with them
two hundred and seventy pieces of artillery.

[4] The main body, under Stuart, had gone around the rear of the
Union army, by Lee's permission, in the expectation of harassing it
while on the march, and of then rejoining Ewell, on the Susquehanna.
It failed to do either, and many attribute all of Lee's misfortunes in this
campaign to the absence of Stuart.

⁵ Jenkins, who commanded, was paid in his own coin at Chambersburg, by the proffer of Confederate scrip in payment for some alleged stolen horses. He himself had been professedly paying for certain seized property in this same worthless scrip.

⁶ Contrast this with the generous, even prodigal, way the Union soldiers were provided for, and who can doubt the devotion of these ragged Confederates to their cause?

⁷ So long as this division remained at York, the question as to where Lee meant to concentrate would be still further confused. See diagram.

⁸ Early levied a contribution on the borough, which the town council evaded by pleading poverty.

⁹ A small Union force which had been holding the bridge set it on fire on the approach of the Confederates.

¹⁰ This was Colonel Freemantle, who has a good word for everything Confederate. On being courteously received within the Union lines after Gettysburg, he was much surprised to find that the officers were gentlemen.

III

FIRST EFFECTS OF THE INVASION

MEANTIME, from before and behind the Confederate columns, two streams flowed out of the doomed valley: one to the north, an army of fugitives hurrying their flocks, herds, and household goods out of the enemy's reach; the other carrying off to Virginia the plunder of towns and villages.

As the swarm of fugitives made straight for Harrisburg, it was but natural that the inpouring of such panic-stricken throngs, all declaring that the enemy was close behind them, should throw Harrisburg alarmed. that city into the wildest commotion, which every hour tended to increase. We will let an eye-witness describe the events of a single day.

"The morning broke upon a populace all astir, who had been called out of bed by the beat of the alarming drum, the blast of the bugle, and the clanging of bells. The streets were lively with men, who were either returning from a night's work on the fortifications or going over to relieve those who were toiling there. As the sun rose higher the excitement gathered head. All along the streets were omnibuses, wagons, and wheelbarrows, taking in trunks and valuables and rushing them down to the dépôt to be shipped out of rebel range. The stores, the female seminaries, and almost every private residence were busy all of the forenoon in swelling the mountain of freight that lay at the dépôt. Every horse was impressed into service and every porter groaned beneath his burdens.

"The scene at the dépôts was indescribable, if not disgraceful. A sweltering mass of humanity People desert thronged the platforms, all furious to the City.   escape from the doomed city. At the bridge and across the river the scene was equally exciting. All through the day a steady stream of people, on foot and in wagons, young and old, black and white, was pouring across it from the Cumberland Valley, bearing with them their household goods and live-stock. Endless trains, laden

with flour, grain, and merchandise, hourly emerged
from the valley and thundered across the bridge
and through the city. Miles of retreating bag-
gage-wagons, filled with calves and sheep tied together, and great, old-fashioned furnace-wagons
loaded with tons of trunks and boxes, defiled in
continuous procession down the 'pike and across
the river, raising a dust as far as the eye could
see."

It may be added that the records of the State
and the money in the bank-vaults were also re-
moved to places of safety, and the construc-
Precautions   tion of defensive works was begun, as
taken.   much, perhaps, with the purpose of
allaying the popular excitement as from any hope
of holding the city against Lee, since Harrisburg
was in no condition either to stand a siege or
repel an assault at this time.

The wave of invasion made itself felt even as
far as Pittsburg on the one side and Baltimore on
the other.[1] Governor Curtin promptly called on
the people of Pennsylvania to arm and repel the
invader. Yet neither the imminence of the danger nor the stirring appeal of the executive of the

State could arouse them at first. In the emergency the neighboring States were appealed to for help. In response the militia of those States were soon hastening toward the threatened points [2] by every available route; yet it was only too evident that raw soldiers, no matter how zealous or patriotic, would prove little hinderance to Lee's marching where he would, or long dispute with his veterans the possession of Harrisburg were it once seriously attacked.

Militia hurried to Harrisburg.

But where was the army of the Potomac all this time—the army whose special task it was to stand between this invader and his prey? Must unarmed citizens be called upon to arise and defend their homes when a hundred thousand veterans were in the field?

For more than a week Lee had thus been laying waste a most rich and fertile section of Pennsylvania at his leisure. Practically, indeed, the whole State was in his grasp. Would Harrisburg or Philadelphia be the first fruits of his audacity? The prize was indeed tempting, the way open. The only real impediment was the

Army of the Potomac, and Lee, too, was now anxiously asking himself what had become of that army.[3] He had foreseen that it must follow him up; that every effort would be bent to compass his destruction; and it was a foregone conclusion that he must fight somewhere, if there was either enterprise or courage left on the Union side. He had even calculated on drawing the Union army

Lee mystified.   so far away from fortified places that its defeat would ensure the fall of Baltimore and Washington. But as regarding its whereabouts at the present moment, Lee was completely in the dark. In an evil hour he had allowed the bulk of his cavalry to run off on a wild-goose chase around the rear of the Federal army, so that now, in his hour of need, though without his knowing it, the whole Federal army interposed to prevent its return.[4]   It is quite true that up to this time Stuart, who led this cavalry,

His Cavalry   had given so many signal proofs of his
absent.   dexterity that Lee was perhaps justified in inferring that if he heard nothing from Stuart, it was because the Union army was still in Virginia.   And in that belief he was acting.

Moreover, instead of being among a population eager to give him every scrap of information, Lee was now among one where every man, woman, and child was a spy on his own movements. In the absence, then, of definite knowledge touching the Union army, he decided to march on Harrisburg with his whole force, and issued orders accordingly.

Among Spies.

When there was no longer a shadow of doubt that Lee's whole army was on the march up the Cumberland Valley, sweeping that valley clean as it went, the Union army also crossed the Potomac, on the 25th and 26th of June, and at once began moving up east of South Mountain, so as to discharge the double duty laid upon it all along of keeping between the enemy and Washington, while at the same time feeling for him through the gaps of South Mountain as it marched. For this task the Union general kept his cavalry well in hand, instead of letting it roam about at will in quest of adventures.

Union Army crosses the Potomac.

This order of march threw the left wing out as far as Boonsborough and Middletown, with

Buford's cavalry division watching the passes by which the enemy would have to defile, should he think of making an attack from that flank.[5]   The rest of the army was halted, for the moment, around Frederick. The plan of operations, as first fixed, did not lack in boldness or originality. It was to follow Lee up the Cumberland Valley with two corps, numbering twenty thousand men, while the rest of the army should continue its march toward the enemy on the east side of South Mountain, but within supporting distance. As this would be doing just what Lee [6] had most reason to dread, it would seem most in accordance with the rules of war. At any rate, it initiated a vigorously aggressive campaign.

Hooker's Plan.

At this critical moment the Union army was, most unexpectedly, deprived of its head.

In its pursuit of Lee this army had been much hampered by divided counsels, when, if ever united counsels were imperatively called for, now was the time. Worse still, it had too many commanders, both civil and military. The President, the Cabinet, the General-in-Chief (Halleck), and

even some others, in addition to the actual commander, not to speak of the newspa-
pers, had all taken turns in advising or
suggesting what should, or what should not, be
done. United action, sincere and generous co-
operation, as between government and army, were
therefore unattainable here. The government did
not trust its general: the general respected the
generalship of the Cabinet most when it was
silent. Nobody in authority seemed willing to
grant Hooker what he asked for, let it be ever so
reasonable, or permit him to carry out his own
plans unobstructed, were they ever so promising
or brilliant. He could not get the fifteen or
twenty thousand soldiers who were then dawdling
about the camps at Baltimore, Washington, and
Alexandria. He was brusquely snubbed when he
asked for leave to break up the post at Harper's
Ferry, when by doing so ten thousand good
troops would have been freed to act against the
enemy's line of retreat.

Hooker is thwarted.

Harmony being impossible, Lee seemed likely
to triumph through the dissensions of his enemies.
Mortified at finding himself thus distrusted and

overruled, Hooker threw up the command on the 27th, and on the 28th General Meade succeeded him. So suddenly was the change brought about, that when the officer bearing the order awakened Meade out of a sound sleep at midnight, he thought he was being put in arrest.

And leaves the Army.

It is asserted by those who had the best means of knowing—indeed, it is difficult to see how it could be otherwise—that the army had lost faith in Hooker, and that the men were asking of each other, "Are we going to have another Chancellorsville?" Be that as it may, there were few better soldiers in that army than Meade; none, perhaps, so capable of uniting it at this particular juncture, when unity was so all-important and yet so lamentably deficient. This was the third general the army had known within six months, and the seventh since its formation. It was truly the graveyard of generals; and each of the disgraced commanders had his following. If, under these conditions, the Army of the Potomac could still maintain its efficiency unimpaired, it must have been made of different stuff from most armies.

Spirit of the Army.

It was not that the Union soldiers feared to meet Lee's veterans. Lee might beat the generals, but the soldiers—never! Yet it can hardly be doubted that repeated defeat had more or less unsettled their faith in their leaders, if not in themselves; since even the gods themselves struggle in vain against stupidity. [7]

If the new appointment did not silence all jealousies among the generals, or infuse great enthusiasm into the rank and file,—and we are bound to admit that Meade's was not a name to General conjure with,—it is difficult to see how Meade. a better selection could have been made, all things considered. In point of fact, there was no one of commanding ability to appoint; but every man in the army felt that Meade would do his best, and that Meade at his best would not fall far behind the best in the field.

Meade could not become the idol of his soldiers, like Lee, because he was not gifted by nature with that personal magnetism which attracts men without their knowing why; but he could and did command unhesitating obedience and respect.

In point of discipline, however, the Union army

was vastly the superior of its adversary, and that counts for much; and in spite of some friction Best-disci- here and there, like a well-oiled ma-plined Army. chine the army was now again in motion, with a cool head and steady hand to guide it on. But as no machine is stronger than its weakest part, it remained to be seen how this one would bear the strain.

Thus a triumphant and advancing enemy was being followed by a beaten and not over-confident one, its wounds scarcely healed,[8] not much stronger than its opponent, and led by a general new to his place, against the greatest captain of the Confederacy. How could the situation fail to impose caution upon a general so fully and so recently impressed with the consequences of taking a false step? Meade's every move shows that from the beginning this thought was uppermost in his mind.

With the effects of Lee's simple presence thus laid before us, it is entirely safe to ask what should have stopped this general from dictating his own terms of peace, either in Philadelphia or Baltimore, provided he could first beat the Union army in Pennsylvania?

[1] At Pittsburg defensive works were begun. In Philadelphia all business was suspended, and work vigorously pushed on the fortifications begun in the suburbs. At Baltimore the impression prevailed that Lee was marching on that city. The alarm bells were rung, and the greatest consternation prevailed.

[2] A great lukewarmness in the action of the people of Pennsylvania is testified to on all sides. See Professor Jacobs' "Rebel Invasion," etc. About sixteen thousand men of the New York State militia were sent to Harrisburg between the 16th of June and the 3d of July; also several thousand from New Jersey (but ordered home on the 22d). General Couch was put in command of the defences of Harrisburg.

[3] Hooker would not cross the Potomac until assured that Lee's whole army was across. He kept the Blue Ridge between himself and Lee in obedience to his orders to keep Washington covered.

[4] The presence of Lee's cavalry would have allowed greater latitude to his operations, distressed the Pennsylvanians more, and enabled Lee to select his own fighting-ground.

[5] So long as these passes were securely held, Lee would be shut up in his valley.

[6] Open to serious objections; but then, so are all plans. Tied down by his orders, Hooker would have taken some risks for the sake of some great gains. By closing every avenue of escape, it would have ensured Lee's utter ruin, provided he could have been as badly beaten as at Gettysburg.

[7] This feeling was so well understood at Washington that a report was spread among the soldiers that McClellan, their old commander, was again leading them, and the report certainly served its purpose.

[8] The army was not up to its highest point of efficiency. It had just lost fifty-eight regiments by expiration of service. This circumstance was known to Lee. The proportion of veterans was not so great as in the Confederate army, or the character of the new enlistments as high as in 1861 and 1862.

I V

REYNOLDS

THE problem presented to Meade's mind, on taking command, was this: What are the enemy's plans, and where shall I strike him? He knew

Meade's
Problem.

that part of Lee's army was at Chambersburg, part at Carlisle, and part at York. Was it Lee's purpose to concentrate his army upon the detachment at York or upon that at Carlisle, or would he draw these two detachments back into the Cumberland Valley, there to play a merely defensive game? Should the junction be at Carlisle, it would mean an attack on Harrisburg: if at York, or at some point between the main body and York, it would indicate an advance in force toward Philadelphia, Baltimore, or Washington. As all these things were possible, all must be duly weighed and guarded against. With a wily, brave, and confident enemy before him, Meade did not find himself on a bed of roses, truly; and he may well be pardoned the remark attributed to him when ordered to take the command, that he was being led to execution.

Meade needed no soothsayer to tell him that if Lee crossed the mountains, it would be because he meant to fight his way toward his object through every obstacle.

What was that object?

In answering this question the political considerations must be first weighed. In short, the purpose—the great purpose—of the invasion must be penetrated. That being done, the military problem would easily solve itself.

It was not to be supposed that Lee had invaded Pennsylvania solely for the purpose of taking a few small towns, or even a large one, like Harrisburg, or of filling up his depleted magazines. He was evidently after larger game. His ultimate aim, clearly, was to capture Washington, as a signal defeat of the Union army would easily enable him to do. It would crown the campaign brilliantly, would fulfil the hopes, and beyond doubt or cavil ensure the 'triumph, of the Confederacy. It is true that Meade's orders held him down to a defence of the national capital first and foremost; in no sense, then, was he the master of his own acts: yet he showed none the less sagacity, we think, in concluding that Lee would presently be found on the east side of the mountains, and in preparing to meet him there, not astride the mountains as Hooker had proposed doing, but with his whole army more within his reach. Meade was prudent. He would err, if at all, on that side; yet the result vindicated his judgment sooner than was thought for.

This being settled, there still remained the question of relieving Pennsylvania. The enemy's presence there was an indignity keenly enough felt on all sides, but to none was it such a home-thrust as to the Pennsylvanians in the Union army, at the head of whom was Meade himself.[1]

Though Hooker's plan promised excellent results here, Meade was fearful lest Lee should cross the Susquehanna, and take Harrisburg before he could be stopped. To prevent this Meade's the army must be pushed forward. Plans. Meade, therefore, at once drew back the left wing toward Frederick, thus giving up that plan in favor of one which he himself had formed; namely, of throwing the army out more to the northeast, the better to cover Baltimore from attack, should that be Lee's purpose, as Meade more than suspected. Selecting Westminster, therefore, as his base from this time forth, and the line of Big Pipe Creek, a little to the north of that place, as his battle-ground, Meade now set most of the army in motion in that direction, leaving Frederick to the protection of a rear-guard.

The army now marched with its left wing thrown forward toward South Mountain, Buford's cavalry toward Fairfield, to clear that flank, the Left Flank Forward. First and Eleventh Corps toward Emmettsburg, the Third and Twelfth toward Middleburg, the Fifth to Taneytown, the Right Flank refused. Second to Uniontown, and the Sixth, on the extreme right, to New Windsor.

Two other divisions of Union cavalry, Kilpatrick's and Gregg's, marched one on the right flank, the other in front, with orders to keep the front and flanks of the army well scouted and protected.

It will be seen from this order of march that, in proportion as they went forward, Buford's cavalry, with the three infantry corps forming the left wing, were approaching the enemy's main body at Chambersburg. South Mountain was, therefore, the wall behind which the two contending armies were playing at hide-and-seek. [2]

Lee had only just given orders for his whole force to move on Harrisburg, when, late in the night of the 28th, a scout brought news to him of Lee hears Meade is coming. the Union army being across the Potomac, and on the march toward South Mountain. [3] This report could not fail to throw the Confederate headquarters into a fever of excitement, ignorant to that hour of that army's being across the Potomac. The mystery was cleared up at last. In a moment the plan of campaign was changed. [4] Lee soon said to some of the officers about him, "To-morrow, gentlemen, we will not move to Harrisburg as we expected, but will go over to Gettysburg and see what General Meade is about."

By placing himself on the direct road to Baltimore, Lee's purpose of first drawing the Union army away from his line of retreat, and of then assailing it on its own, stands fully revealed. The previous orders were therefore countermanded on the spot. Hill and Longstreet were ordered from

March on Gettysburg begun.

Chambersburg to Gettysburg,[5] Ewell was called back from Carlisle, and Early from York.

If Meade had known Lee's whereabouts, it is safe to assume that the Union army would have

Faulty Tactics.

been massed toward its left rather than its right; and if Lee had been correctly informed on his part, it is unlikely that he would have risked throwing his columns out at random against the Union army, as he was now doing. Only the fatuity of the Union generals saved Lee's vanguard on the 1st of July. Yet he held the very important advantage of having already begun the concentration of his army—an easy thing for him to do, inasmuch as but one of his three corps was separated from the others— before Meade discovered by chance what was so near proving his ruin. One day's march would bring all three up within supporting distances, two in position for giving battle.

Heth's division of Hill's Corps got as far as Cashtown, eight miles from Gettysburg, on the 29th; Rodes' division of Ewell's Corps was coming down by the direct road from Carlisle, east of South Mountain; Early's division of this corps began its march back from York to Gettysburg on the morning of the 30th. These three divisions, or one-third of Lee's whole army, therefore, formed the enemy's vanguard which would first strike an approaching force. But, as we have seen, the whole army was in march behind it, and by the next day well closed up on the advance.

Confederate Positions June 29th.

Leaving them to pursue their march, which was by no means hurried, let us, to borrow Lee's very expressive phrase, "see what General Meade was about."

On the 29th all seven of the Union corps were advancing northward like fingers spread apart, and exactly in an inverse order from Lee's three, which were converging on the palm of the hand. On the 30th this divergent order of march continued to conduct the corps still farther apart, with the result also,

Union Positions June 30th.

considering Gettysburg as the ultimate point of concentration, that the bulk of the army was away off to the right of Gettysburg.[6]   Moreover, Meade's efforts to get the army up to this position, or in front of his chosen line of defence on Pipe Creek, had covered the roads with stragglers, and compelled at least one corps to halt for nearly a whole day.[7]

It was not until nightfall of the 30th, or forty-eight hours after it was begun, that Meade knew of the enemy's movement toward Gettysburg; and even then he did not feel at all sure of having detected the true point of concentration. Indeed, his want of accurate information on this head seems surprising. By that time his own army was stretched out from Emmettsburg, on the northwest, to Manchester at the east, thus putting Scattered Condition of the Army. it out of Meade's power to concentrate it at Gettysburg in one day. By endeavoring to cover too much ground his army had been dangerously scattered. Even without cavalry Lee had fairly stolen a march on him. And it is not improbable that Hooker might now have been "shocked," in his turn.[8]

Our present business is now wholly with the left wing of the Union army,—its right being quite out of reach,—that is to say, with the three infantry and one cavalry corps commanded by that thorough soldier, so beloved by the whole army, General Reynolds, the actual chief of the First Corps.

Union Left Wing in Advance.

Buford had spent the 29th in scouring the passes of South Mountain as far north as Monterey, without getting sight of the enemy, however, until he halted for the night at Fountaindale, when he then perceived the camp-fires of a numerous body of troops stretching along in his front and lighting up the road toward Gettysburg. Evidently they had just crossed South Mountain from the valley.

Buford finds the Enemy.

To Buford this sight was indeed as a ray of light in a dark place. No friendly force could be in that quarter. He determined to know who and what it was without loss of time. Before dawn his troopers were again in the saddle. They soon fell in with a strong column of infantry moving toward Gettysburg on the Fairfield (Hagerstown) road. After exchanging a

He attacks.

few shots, and having learned what he wanted to know, Buford hastened back to Reynolds, at Emmettsburg, with the news.

Reynolds immediately sent Buford back to Gettysburg, in order, if possible, to head off the enemy before he should reach that place, for which he was evidently making. A courier was also despatched to headquarters. This was the first trustworthy intelligence of Lee's movement to the east that Meade had thus far received. Could the enemy be massing on his left? It certainly looked like it. After this night there was only one word on the tongues of all men in that army—Gettysburg! Gettysburg!

The First Corps, also marching for Gettysburg, went into camp some five miles short of that town; the Eleventh lay at Emmettsburg; the Third at Taneytown. It is with them alone that we shall have to deal in what follows.

Reynolds marches up.

We have already seen that Meade had not designed advancing one step farther than might be found effectual for turning Lee back from overrunning the State. This was the first great

object to be attained. And this had now been
done. To avoid being struck from behind, Lee
had been forced to halt, face about, and look for

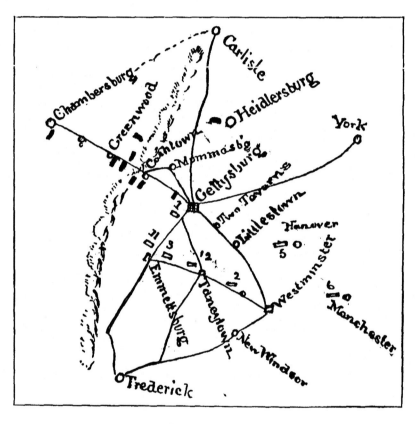

Positions, June 30th.

a place to fight in. When the enemy should
be fairly in motion southward, Meade meant

to take up the position along Pipe Creek, and
await an attack there. But he no
longer had the disposing of events
In order to gain this position now, Reynolds
must have fallen back one or two marches; nor
could Meade know that Lee was then coming half
way to meet him; or that—strange confusion of
ideas!—Lee had promised his generals not to fight
a pitched battle except on ground of his own
choosing; certainly not on one his adversary
had chosen for him; least of all where defeat
would carry down with it the cause of the
Southern Confederacy itself.

Reynolds, therefore, held the destinies of both
armies in his keeping on that memorable last
night of June. He now knew that any
further advance on his part would probably result in bringing on a combat—a combat,
moreover, in which both armies might become involved, for his military instinct truly foreshadowed
what was coming. There was still time to fall
back on the main army, to avoid an engagement.
But Reynolds was not that kind of general. He
was the man of all others to whom the whole

army had looked in the event of Hooker's incapacity from any cause, as well as the first whom
the President had designed to replace him.
He now shared Meade's confidence to the fullest
extent. He was a soldier of the finest temper,
a Pennsylvanian, like Meade himself, neither
rash on the one hand, nor weighed down by
the feeling that he or his soldiers were over-
matched in any respect on the other. To him,
at least, Lee was no bugbear. Having come
there expressly to find the enemy, he was not
going to turn his back now that the enemy was
found. Reynolds was, therefore, emphatically the
man for the hour. He knew that Meade would
support him to the last man and the last cartridge.
He fall back? There was no such word in Reynolds' vocabulary. His order was "Forward!"

So history has indissolubly linked together
the names of Reynolds and of Gettysburg, for
had he decided differently there would have been
no battle of Gettysburg.

Thus it was that all through the silent watches
of that moonlit summer's night the roads leading to Gettysburg from north and south, from east

and west, were lighted up by a thousand camp-
fires. Without knowing it, the citizens of that
peaceful village were sleeping on a volcano,

[1] Besides Meade, there were Hancock, Reynolds, and Humphreys—
a triumvirate of some power with that army. Pennsylvania had also
seventy-three regiments and five batteries with Meade.

[2] While thus feeling for Lee along the mountain passes with his left
hand, Meade was reaching out the right as far as possible toward the
Susquehanna, or toward Early at York.

[3] This was Longstreet's scout, Harrison. "He said there were
three corps near Frederick when he passed there, one to the right and
one to the left; but he did not succeed in getting the position of the
other."—*Longstreet.*

[4] This shows how little foundation exists for the statements of the
Comte de Paris and others that Hooker's strategy compelled Lee to
cross the mountain, when it is clear that he knew nothing whatever of
Hooker's intentions. This is concurred in by both Lee and Longstreet. Moreover, Hooker had scarcely put his strategy in effect when
he was relieved.

[5] In point of fact, the concentration was first ordered for Cashtown,
" at the eastern base of the mountain."—*Lee.* Ewell and Hill took the
responsibility of going on to Gettysburg, after hearing that the Union
cavalry had been seen there.

[6] On the night of June 30th, Meade's headquarters and the artillery
reserve were at Taneytown, the First Corps at Marsh Run, Eleventh
at Emmettsburg, Third at Bridgeport, Twelfth at Littlestown, Second at
Uniontown, Fifth at Union Mills, Sixth and Gregg's Cavalry at Manchester, Kilpatrick's at Hanover—a line over thirty miles long.

[7] By being compelled to ford streams without taking off shoes or
stockings, the men's feet were badly blistered.

[8] Upon taking command, Meade is said to have expressed himself
as "shocked" at the scattered condition of the army.

V

THE FIRST OF JULY

SINCE early in the afternoon of June 30th, the inhabitants of Gettysburg had seen pouring through their village, taking position on the heights that dominate it, and spread-

Buford.

ing themselves out over all the roads leading into it from the west and north, squadron after squadron of horse, dusty and travel-stained, but alert, vigilant, and full of ardor at the prospect of coming to blows with the enemy at last.

This was a portion of that splendid cavalry which, under the lead of Pleasonton, Buford, Gregg, and Kilpatrick, at last disputed the boasted superiority of Stuart's famous troopers. At last the Union army had a cavalry force. These men formed the van of that army which was pursuing Lee by forced marches for the purpose of bringing him to battle.

Forewarned that he must look for the enemy

to make his appearance on the Chambersburg and Carlisle roads,[1] and feeling that there was warm work ahead, Buford was keeping a good lookout in both directions. To that end he had now Oak Ridge. taken post on a commanding ridge over which these roads passed first to Seminary Ridge, and so back into Gettysburg. First causing his troopers to dismount, he formed them across the two roads in question in skirmishing order, threw out his vedettes, planted his horse-artillery, and with the little valley of Willoughby Run. Willoughby Run before him, the Seminary and Gettysburg behind him, and the First Corps in bivouac only five miles away toward Emmettsburg, this intrepid soldier calmly awaited the coming of the storm, conscious that if Gettysburg was to be defended at all it must be from these heights.

A pretty little valley was this of Willoughby Run, with its green banks and clear-flowing waters, its tall woods and tangled shrubbery, so soon to be torn and defaced by shot and shell, so soon deformed by drifting smoke and the loud cries of the combatants.

The night passed off quietly. Nevertheless, some thirty thousand Confederates, of all arms, were lying in camp within a radius of eight miles from Gettysburg. Their vanguard had discovered the presence of our cavalry,[2] and was waiting for the morning only to brush it away.

Next morning Heth's division was marching down the Chambersburg pike, looking for this cavalry, when its advance fell in with Buford's vedettes. While they halted to reconnoitre, these vedettes came back with the news that the enemy was advancing in force, infantry and artillery filling the road as far as could be seen. Warned that not a moment was to be lost, Buford at once sent off word to Reynolds, who, after ordering the First Corps under arms, and sending back for the Eleventh, himself set off at a gallop for Gettysburg, followed only by his staff.

Heth comes down the Pike.

Buford's bold front had thus caused the enemy to come to a halt; but soon after nine, supposing he had to do with cavalry alone, Heth deployed his skirmishers across the pike, forming his two leading brigades at each side

He drives Buford.

of it; these troops then pushed forward, and soon the crack of a musket announced that the battle of Gettysburg had begun.

After an hour's stubborn fighting, Buford was being slowly but surely pushed back over the first ridge, when a column of the Union infantry was seen coming up the Emmettsburg road at the

Wadsworth comes to Buford's Aid.

double-quick. It was Wadsworth's division arriving in the nick of time, as the enemy's skirmishers, followed by Archer's brigade, were, even then, in the act of fording the run unopposed, and unless promptly stopped would soon be in possession of the first range of heights. It was really a neck-and-neck race to see who would get there first.

Reynolds was impatiently awaiting the arrival of his troops, who were making across the fields for the ridge he was so desirous of holding on the run. It was plain as day that he had determined to contest the enemy's possession of Gettysburg here. Cutler's brigade was the first to arrive.

Reynolds forms the Division.

Hurrying this off to the right of the pike, where it formed along the crest of the ridge under a shower of balls,

Reynolds ordered the next, as it came up, to charge on over the ridge in its front, and drive Archer's men out of a wood that rose before him crowning the crest and running down the opposite slopes. It was done in the most gallant manner, Charge of the each regiment in turn breaking off from Iron Brigade. the line of march to join in the charge under the eye of Reynolds himself, who, heedless of everything except the supreme importance of securing the position, rode on after the leading regiment into the fire where bullets were flying thickest. Not only was the enemy driven out of the wood, but back across the run, with the loss of about half the brigade, including Archer Reynolds himself. At the very moment success falls. had crowned his first effort, Reynolds fell dead with a bullet in his brain.[3]

Nothing could have been more unfortunate at this time. With Reynolds fell the whole inspiration of the battle of Gettysburg, but, worst of all, Evil Conse- with his fall both the directing mind quences. and that unquestioned authority so essential to bring the battle to a successful issue vanished from the field. He had been struck down too suddenly even to transmit his views to a subordinate. Disaster was in the air.

This dearly bought success on the left was more than offset by what was going on at the right, where Davis' Confederate brigade, after getting
Cutler is   round Cutler's flank, was driving all
driven.   before it. Cutler had to fall back to the Seminary Ridge in disorder.

Having so easily cleared this part of the line, Davis' men next threw themselves astride the ridge, and seeing nothing before them but Hall's battery, which was then firing down the Chambersburg pike, they came booming down upon the guns, yelling like so many Comanche Indians. Before the battery could be limbered up the enemy were among the guns, shooting the cannoneers and bayoneting the horses. It was finally got off with the loss of one of the pieces.[4]

This success put the enemy in possession of all the Union line as far down as the pike, and threatened that part just won with a like fate. We had routed the enemy on the left, and been routed on the right.

Fortunately, the Sixth Wisconsin had been left in reserve near the Seminary a little earlier, and it was now ordered to the rescue. Colonel Dawes led his men up on the run. This regiment, with two of Cutler's that had turned back on see-

The Ridge recovered.

ing the diversion making in their favor, drove the enemy back again, up the ridge, to where it is crossed by a railroad cut, some two hundred yards north of the pike. To escape this attack most of them jumped down into the cut; but as the banks are high and steep and the outlet narrow, this was only getting out of the frying-pan into the fire, since while one body

Davis in a Trap.

of pursuers was firing down into them from above, still another had thrown it-self across the outlet and was raking the cut from end to end. This proved more than even Davis' Mississippians could stand, and though they fought obstinately enough, all were either killed, taken, or dispersed.

Heth's two attacking brigades having thus been practically used up after a fierce conflict, not with cavalry alone, with whom they had expected to have a little fun, but with infantry, in whom they recognized their old antagonists of many a hard-fought field, and who fought to-day with a determination unusual even to them, Heth hesitated about advancing to the attack again in the face of such a check as he had just received, without strong backing up; but sending word of his encounter to Lee, he set about forming the fragments of the two defeated brigades on two fresh ones, where they could be sheltered from the Union fire.

Heth brought to a Standstill.

Yet Hill, his immediate chief, had told him only the night before there was no objection in the world to his going into Gettysburg the next day.

This success also enabled Doubleday[5] to reform his line in its old position. The troops on the left had not been shaken, and Cutler's men were now coming back to the front eager to wipe out the disgrace of their defeat.

If the enemy's van had not been without cavalry to clear its march, Heth must inevitably have got into Gettysburg first. As it was, the unexpected resistance he had met with made Heth cautious. Lee's orders to his lieutenants were not to force the fighting until the whole army should be up. Pender was therefore forming behind Heth, the artillery set at work, and all were impatiently looking out for Rodes' appearance on the Carlisle (or Mummasburg) road, before renewing the action.

This proved a most fortunate respite to the small Union force on Oak Ridge, as, in consequence of it, — the state of things just pointed out, — some hours elapsed before there was any more fighting by the infantry, though the artillery kept up its annoying fire. Meanwhile the two remaining divisions of the First Corps came on the ground. Robinson's was left in reserve at the Seminary, with orders to throw up some breastworks there; Doubleday's, now Rowley's, went into line partly to the right and partly to the left of the troops already there, thus extending both flanks considerably; and at the extreme left, which was held by Biddle's brigade, two companies of the Twentieth New York were even thrown out across the run, into. the Harman house and out-buildings, where they did good service in keeping down the enemy's skirmish fire. 6

Eleven o'clock.

Meantime, also, Pender's division had got into line. When formed for the attack it considerably outflanked the Union left. And a little later Rodes was seen coming down the Mummasburg road, Rodes on Union Flank. or out quite beyond the right of the First Corps. Clearly, the combat just closed was child's play in comparison with what was about to begin.

These troops gave notice that they were shortly coming into action by opening a sharp cannonade from Oak Hill, the commanding eminence situ- Oak Hill seized. ated just beyond and in fact forming a continuation of Oak Ridge, where the First Corps stood, though separated from it somewhat.

This artillery fire from Oak Hill enfiladed the Union position so completely that nothing was left for the right but to fall back to Seminary Ridge, so as to show a new front to this attack. The centre and left, however, kept its former position, with some rearrangement of the line here and there, which had now become a very crooked one.

Twenty odd thousand men were thus waiting

for the word to rush upon between ten and eleven thousand.

Before the battle could be renewed, however, the Eleventh Union Corps came up through Gettysburg.[7]   Howard, its actual head, was now in chief command of the field, as next in Eleventh Corps rank to Reynolds. He sent forward comes up.   Schurz's and Barlow's divisions of this corps to confront Rodes, leaving Steinwehr's in reserve on Cemetery Hill.

Having preceded his corps to the field, Howard had already notified Meade, too hastily by half, that Reynolds was killed and the First Corps routed — a report only half true, and calculated Howard calls to do much mischief, as it soon spread for Help.   throughout the entire army. He also sent off an urgent request to Slocum, who was halted in front of Two Taverns, not five miles off, to come to his assistance with the Twelfth Corps.

Supposing the day lost from the tenor of Howard's despatch, lacking perhaps the fullest confidence in that general's ability and experience, and thinking only of how he should save what was left, Meade forthwith posted Hancock off to Gettysburg, with full authority to take

Hancock command of all the troops he might
comes to the find there, decide whether Gettysburg
Front. should be held or given up, and to
promptly report his decision, to the end that
proper steps might be taken to counteract this
disaster if yet possible.

Slocum would not stir from Two Taverns without orders, though it is said the firing was distinctly heard there, and he could have reached
Gettysburg in an hour and a half. A second and

Slocum and still more urgent appeal decided that
Sickles. commander, late in the afternoon, to
set his troops in motion. It was then too late.
Sickles, who might have been at Gettysburg
inside of three hours with the greater part of
his corps, appears to have lingered in a deplor-
able state of indecision until between two and
three o'clock in the afternoon, before he could
make up his mind what to do. It was then too
late. [8]

By contrast we find Ewell promptly going to
Hill's assistance upon a simple request for such
coöperation, though Ewell was Hill's senior;

and we further find that his doing so proved
the turning-point of this very battle.

Was there a want of cordiality between the

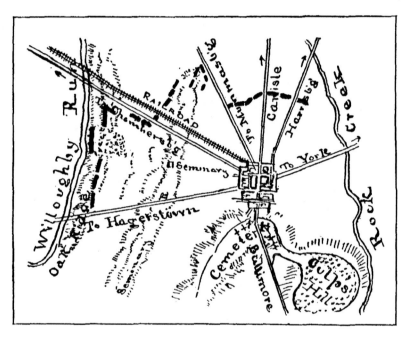

Union Positions, July 1, 3 P.M.

Union commanders? Was it really culpable
negligence, or was there only incapacity?

While, therefore, one corps certainly, two
probably, might easily have got to the field in
season to take a decisive part in the battle, but

remained inactive, the Confederates were hurrying every available man forward to the point
of danger. This was precisely where Reynolds'
fall proved supremely disastrous, and where an
opportunity to acquire a decisive superiority on
the field of battle was most unfortunately thrown
away for want of a head.[9]

The Union line, lengthened out by the arrival
of the Eleventh Corps, had now been carried in
a quarter circle around Gettysburg, or from the
New Union   Hagerstown road on the left to near
Line.   Rock Creek on the right, the Eleventh
Corps being deployed across the open fields
extending from the Mummasburg to the Harrisburg road, with Barlow's division on the extreme
right. When this corps formed front in line of
battle, there was a gap of a quarter of a mile left
wide open between it and the First Corps.
Furthermore, it was drawn up on open ground
which, if not actually level, is freely overlooked
by all the surrounding heights.

That this corps was badly posted was demon-
strated after a very brief trial.

Having got into line facing southward, Rodes

began his advance against the right of the First Corps and left of the Eleventh shortly before

Rodes attacks.

three o'clock, supported by a tremendous artillery fire from Oak Hill. Our troops stood firm against this new onslaught. It was only fairly under way, however, when Heth and Pender joined in the attack.

The fighting now begun was on both sides of the most determined character.

On his side, Rodes was quick to take advantage of the break existing between the two Union corps, and promptly pushed his soldiers into it; but they were not to get possession so easily,

Bloody Fighting.

for Doubleday now ordered up his last division to stem the tide surging in upon his uncovered flank. These troops gallantly rushed into the breach, where a murderous contest began at close quarters, with the result that, failing to close up the gap, the division was finally drawn around the point of the ridge, where the Mummasburg road descends into the plain, so forming a natural bastion from which the Union soldiers now drove back their assailants with great slaughter. Many of Iverson's brigade were literally lying dead in their ranks after this repulse.

In front of Meredith, who still held the wood, and Stone's "Bucktails," who lay at their right, "no rebel crossed the run for one hour and lived." Beyond them Biddle was still holding his own at the left, though his ranks were fast thinning. On both sides the losses were enormous. In twenty-five minutes Heth had lost two thousand seven hundred out of seven thousand men. This division having been fought out, Pender's was brought up, the artillery redoubled its fire, Rodes pushed his five brigades forward again, and a general advance of comparatively fresh troops was begun all along the line.

But it was on the right that disaster first fell with crushing force.

Here Rodes' assault on the left of the Eleventh Corps met stout resistance. But while the troops here were fighting or shifting positions to repel Rodes' rapid blows, Early's division was seen advancing down the Harrisburg road against the right, which it almost immediately struck. Thus reinforced and connected,

Early strikes in.

not quite one-half of Lee's whole army was now closing in around two-sevenths of the Union army.

Obstinate fighting now took place all along the line. The First Corps held out some time longer against repeated assaults, losing men fast, but also inflicting terrible punishment upon their assailants, Rodes alone losing two thousand five hundred men before he could carry the positions before him. The Confederate veterans, though not used to praising their opponents, freely said that the First Union Corps did the fiercest fighting on this day of which they ever had any experience.

But Early's attack on the right, though sternly resisted by Barlow, proved the last straw in this case. The right division being rolled back in disorder by an assault made both in front and flank, the left also gave way in its turn, and soon the His Attack whole corps was in full retreat across is decisive. the fields to the town, which the exultant enemy entered along with them, picking up a great many prisoners on the way or in the streets, notwithstanding a brigade of the reserve came down from Cemetery Hill to check the pursuit.

The Eleventh Corps being thus swept away, the

First fell back rather forsaken than defeated, a few regiments on the left making a final stand at the seminary to enable those on the right to shake off their pursuers. But at last the winding lines came down from Seminary Ridge into the plain. Buford's cavalry again came to the rescue in this part of the field, riding with drawn sabres between pursuers and pursued, so that the Confederates hastily formed some squares to repel a charge, while the wreck of the Union line, disdaining to run, doggedly fell back toward the town, halting now and then to turn and fire a parting volley or rally its stragglers round their colors. It was not hard pushed except at the extreme right, where some of Robinson's division fell into the enemy's hands; nor did resistance cease until its decimated battalions again closed up their ranks on the brow of Cemetery Hill— noble relic of one of the hardest-fought battles of this war. Of the eight thousand two hundred men who had gone into action in the morning, five thousand seven hundred and fifty had been left on the blood-dyed summit of Oak Ridge, or in the enemy's hands. The

All in Retreat.

Union Losses.

losses were frightful. In one brigade alone, one thousand two hundred and three men had fallen. In all, the losses more than equalled half the effective strength.

The Eleventh Corps also lost heavily, though mostly in prisoners. In both corps ten thousand soldiers were missing at roll-call.

Early's soldiers were now swarming about Gettysburg in great spirits. Hays' brigade alone entered the town, Avery going into a field on the East, and the others out on the York road. Rodes presently came up at the west, much disordered from his pursuit of Robinson. These Confederates then set about re-forming their shattered ranks, The Enemy in Gettysburg. under the fire of the Union artillery from Cemetery Hill and of the sharpshooters posted in the houses along its slopes. This fire became so galling that the enemy's infantry were obliged to get under cover of the nearest ridges or houses. In this way Ewell's Corps came to be planted nearest the approaches to Cemetery Hill.

Heth and Pender did not advance beyond Seminary Ridge. They had had fighting enough for one day. [10] Lee was also there examining the new Union position through his glass. Notwithstanding

Heth and
Pender.

the general elation visible about him, the victory did not seem quite complete to Lee so long as the Federals still maintained their defiant attitude at the Cemetery. There was evidently more, and perhaps harder, work ahead.

There is no evading the plain, if unwelcome, truth that this battle had been lost, and two corps of the Union army nearly destroyed, for want of a little more decision when decision was most urgently called for, and a little more energy when activity was all-important. The fate of most great battles has been decided by an hour or two, more or less. Two of indecision decided this one.

[1] Buford's information was quite exact. "June 30, 10.30 P.M. I am satisfied that A.P. Hill's corps is massed just back of Cashtown, about nine miles from this place. Pender's division of this corps came up to-day, of which I advised you. The enemy's pickets, infantry and artillery, are within four miles of this place, at the Cashtown road."– *Buford to Reynolds.*

[2] Colonel Chapman Biddle puts the Confederate force in camp around Cashtown or Heidlersburg, each eight miles from Oak Ridge, at thirty-five thousand of all arms; perhaps rather an over-estimate of this careful writer.

[3] His horse carried him a short distance onward before he fell. His

body was carried to the rear, in a blanket, just as Archer was being brought in a prisoner.

[4] When attacked in this way a battery is at the mercy of its assailants.

[5] General Abner Doubleday succeeded to the command of the First Corps on Reynolds' death.

[6] The First Corps finally held a line of about a mile and a half, from the Hagerstown to the Mummasburg road.

[7] The head of this corps arrived at about 12.45 and the rear at 1.45 P.M. It would take not less than an hour to get it into position from a half to three-fourths of a mile out of Gettysburg.

[8] It is a well-settled principle of war as well as of common sense that a corps commander may disregard his orders whenever their literal execution would be in his opinion unwarranted by conditions unknown to, or unforeseen by, the general in command of the army when he issued them. This refers, of course, to an officer exercising a separate command, and not when in the presence of his superior.

[9] The positions of the several corps that afternoon were as follows, except the First and Eleventh: Second at Taneytown, Third at Emmettsburg, Fifth at Hanover, Sixth at Manchester, and Twelfth at Two Taverns.

[10] Heth, Rodes, and Early admit a loss of five thousand eight hundred without counting prisoners. The prisoners taken by the First Corps would swell this number to about eight thousand.

VI

CEMETERY HILL

W E have seen Lee arriving on the field his troops had carried just as ours were streaming over Cemetery Hill in his plain sight. Seeing

Lee wants to push Things. Ewell already established within gunshot of this hill, Lee wished him to push on after the fugitives, seize Cemetery Hill, and so reap all the fruits of the victory just won.

Ewell hesitated, and the golden opportunity slipped through Lee's fingers. At four o'clock he would have met with little resistance: at six it was different.

By riding hard, Hancock[1] got to Gettysburg soon after Lee did. The road leading from the

Hancock arrives. battlefield was thronged with fugitives, wounded men, ammunition wagons, and ambulances, all hurrying to the rear (the unmistakable débris of a routed army), as Hancock spurred up Cemetery Hill. His trained eye took in the situation at a glance. Everywhere he saw Finds Situation gloomy. the gloom of defeat. A few disordered battalions sullenly clung around their colors, but the men seemed stunned and disheartened, not so much by defeat as by the palpable fact that they had been abandoned to defeat for want of a scrap of paper, more or less. Instead of cheers, set faces and haggard eyes greeted Hancock as he rode along the diminished ranks. He saw divisions reduced to brigades; brigades to battalions; battalions to companies; batteries to a single gun. One of Steinwehr's brigades and some of his batteries, with a regiment of the First Corps that had not been in action,[2] was the only force remaining intact. These guns were sending an occasional shot down into the streets of Gettysburg; while more to the left—cheering sight!—Buford's cavalry stood drawn up before the heights steady as on parade, first in the field and last out of it.

Hancock's animating presence gradually put heart into the men. He saw just what ought to be done, and instantly set about doing it.

A swift and comprehensive view of the ground—
and his grasp of its capabilities was singularly just
—seems to have convinced Hancock that no better
place to fight in was likely to be found, even
Order is   should the enemy allow them the time
restored.   to concentrate in the rear, which was
become the all-important question just then. He
gave his orders rapidly, broken ranks were re-
formed, fugitives brought back to their colors,[3]
the tide of retreat stayed. As the last gun
was fired from Cemetery Hill, Stannard's Vermont brigade[4] came marching up the Emmettsburg road, and was at once put in line south
First Rein-   of the Cemetery, with pickets thrown
forcements.   out in front. Though small, this re-
inforcement was thrice welcome at a time when
it could not be known whether the enemy would
attack or not, and it had a good effect.

In riding up, Hancock had not failed to notice—
indeed, no one could—a wooded hill standing off at
some distance to the right of Cemetery Hill, from
                  which it was separated by a wide and
Culp's Hill.   deep hollow, yet at the same time
joined by a ridge so low and narrow as to be

hardly seen when looking down from above. This low, connecting ridge is several hundred yards in extent, and, forming as it does a natural parapet for infantry, was all that stood in the way of pushing a force through between Cemetery and Culp's Hill to the rear of the Union troops. Of the two hills it is enough to say that as Culp's Hill is much the higher, whoever held Culp's Hill would also hold the key to the Union position, as Hancock found it.

Commands Cemetery.

The enemy had not been slow to perceive this on his part, and while hesitating what to do Early had pointed it out to Ewell, his chief, who fully agreed with him that it should be seized as soon as Johnson's fresh division got up.[5] But while they were hesitating Hancock was sending what was left of Wadsworth's division, reinforced by the Seventh Indiana, with a battery, to occupy Culp's Hill; so that when Johnson's scouts went there after dark, instead of finding the hill unoccupied and undefended, they fell into the hands of Wadsworth's men. Meredith's worn but undaunted brigade dropped into position behind the narrow strip of ridge spoken

Ewell sees it too.

of, a sure guaranty that no enemy would break
But Hancock seizes it. through at that place. In this instance
Hancock's eagle glance and no less
prompt action undoubtedly saved the whole
position, since if Ewell had succeeded in estab-
lishing himself on Gulp's Hill, it would have
taken the whole Union army to drive him out.

Considered merely as a rallying point for
broken troops, Cemetery Hill had now served its
purpose. Hancock could now say to Meade,
not that the position was the best they could have
taken for disputing the enemy's progress, but that
Hancock reports all safe. all was safe for the present, or equally
in train for the withdrawal of the
troops, should that be the decision.
In a word, he would not commit himself unreserv-
edly to a simple yes or no.[6]

It was now Meade's turn, and right nobly did
he rise to the crisis. Such as it was, Hancock's
report enabled him to come to a quick decision.
Instead of ordering a retreat, he instantly ordered
Meade's Decision. all the corps to Gettysburg. From the
moment he became satisfied that there
was a fighting chance in front, Meade's conduct

was anything but that of a defeated or even timid general; he seems never to have looked behind him. Had he been so unalterably wedded to his own chosen line of defence as some critics profess to believe, it is difficult to see what stronger excuse could have offered itself for falling back than the defeat he had just suffered. And if he had shrunk from the hazard of fighting so far from his base before, how much more easily could he have justified his refusal to do so after the loss of ten thousand men, the sudden disruption of his plans, with the increased sense of responsibility all this involved! We think few would deny that the bringing up of four-sevenths of the army over distances varying from thirteen to thirty-six miles must appear a far bolder act, even to the unmilitary mind, than causing three-sevenths to fall back some fifteen miles. Fortunately Meade was one in spirit with his soldiers, who with one voice demanded to be led against the enemy. The shock of battle seems to have aroused all the warrior's instinct within him. Reynolds may have forced the fighting, Hancock suggested, or even advised, but it was Meade, and

Meade alone, on whose deliberate judgment the battle of Gettysburg was renewed, and who therefore stands before history as its undoubted sponsor.

To return to the now historic Cemetery Hill. Here the right, reinforced by at least three thousand fresh troops,[7] had been strongly occupied. Everything appeared in surety on this side. But all the way from the Taneytown Road to Little Round Top there was not one solitary soldier or gun except some cavalry pickets. By the time, however, that Hancock had succeeded in bringing order out of this chaos and courage out of despair, the whole situation was changed by the arrival of the Twelfth Corps from Two Taverns. Twelfth Corps comes up, 5 P.M. As it came up by the Baitimore pike the leading division (Williams') turned off to the right, feeling its way out in this direction as far as Wolf's Hill and the Hanover road; but on finding the enemy already installed on that side, the division was massed for the night on the Baltimore pike, so rendering secure our extreme right at Culp's Hill. There was no longer anything to apprehend on this side. We cannot refrain from asking what would have been the effect of the appearance of these troops on Early's flank an hour or two earlier in the afternoon?

Geary's division of this corps having kept straight on up the pike to Cemetery Hill, Hancock turned it off to the extreme left, partly to make some show in that as yet unguarded quarter, about which he felt by no means easy, partly to hold control of the Emmettsburg and Taneytown roads (see map), by which more of the Union troops were marching to the field. Stretching itself out in a thin line as far as Little Round Top, and after sending one regiment out on picket toward the Emmettsburg road, and just to the right of the Devil's Den, the division slept on its arms, in a position destined to become celebrated, first on account of Hancock's foresight in seizing it, next by reason of its desertion by the general intrusted with its defence.

Geary at Little Round Top.

Fix this on the Map.

Hancock had the satisfaction of feeling that the position was safe for the present when he rode back to Taneytown, first to meet his own corps on the road, and next to find that the whole army

Second Corps nearly up.
had already been ordered up. Throwing Gibbon an order to halt as he passed, Hancock kept on to headquarters. His work was done.

Nothing but the importance which this critical period of the battle has assumed to our own mind could justify the giving of all these details by which the gradual patching up and lengthening

Union Line at Dark.
out of the line, until it took the form it subsequently held, and from a front of a few hundred yards grew to be two miles long, may be better followed.

As regards the rest of the army, some part of the Third Corps had now reached the ground by

Part of Third corps up.
the Emmettsburg road, though too late to get into line; its pickets, however, were thrown out on that road as far to the left as a cross-road leading

Find Sherfy's on Map,
down from Sherfy's house to Little Round Top. The rest of this corps would come up by this same road in the morning. The Second Corps was halting for the night three miles back, also in a position to

guard the left of the line. Nominally, therefore, five of the seven corps were up at dark that night, Other Corps or at least near enough to go into where? position by daybreak. The Fifth being then at Hanover, twenty-four miles back, and the Sixth, which was the strongest in the army, at Manchester, thirty-five miles from Gettysburg, it still became a question whether the whole Union army could be assembled in season to overcome Lee's superiority on the field.[8]

Indeed, when Meade did finally order the whole Chances army to Gettysburg, the chances were against as ten to one against its getting up in Meade. time to fight as a unit.

Would that portion of the Union forces found on Cemetery Hill on the morning of the second be beaten in detail, as the First and Eleventh had been the day before?

This seems, in fact, to have been Lee's real purpose, as he told Longstreet at five o'clock, when they were looking over the ground together, that if Meade's army was on the heights next day it must be dislodged. Knowing that but two Union corps had been engaged that day against him, Lee seemed impressed with the idea that he could

beat Meade before the rest of his army
could arrive. Longstreet strongly opposed making a direct attack, though without

shaking his chief's purpose. As Lee
now had his whole army well in hand,
one division only being absent,[9] he seemed little
disposed to begin a new series of combinations,
when, in his opinion, he had the Union army half
defeated, half scattered, and wholly at a disad-
vantage. And we think he was right.

We have seen that Lee's conclusions with respect to the force before him were so nearly cor-
rect as to justify his confidence in his own plans.
Ever since crossing South Mountain he had expected a battle. It is true he found it forced
upon him sooner than he expected, yet his own
army had been the first to concentrate, his troops

had gained a partial victory by this
very means, and both general and soldiers were eager to consummate it while the
chances were still so distinctly in their favor.
Even if Lee was somewhat swayed by a belief in
his own genius, as some of his critics have sug-

gested,—a belief which had so far carried him
from victory to victory,—we cannot blame him.
War is a game of chance, and Lee now saw that
chance had put his enemy in his power.

At the close of the day Lee therefore rode over
to see if Ewell could not open the battle by carrying Cemetery Hill. Ewell bluntly declared it
Ewell   to be an impossibility. The Union
says No.   troops, he said, would be at work
strengthening their already formidable positions
there all night, so that by morning they would be
found well-nigh impregnable. Culp's Hill had
been snatched from his grasp. The rugged
character of these heights, the impossibility of
using artillery to support an attack, the exposure
Cemetery Hill of the assaulting columns to the fire
too Strong.   of the Union batteries at short range,
were all forcibly dwelt upon and fully concurred
in by Ewell's lieutenants. In short, so many objections appeared that, willing or unwilling, Lee
found himself forced to give over the design of
breaking through the Union line at this point and
taking the road to Baltimore.

It was then suggested that the attack should

begin on the Union left, where, to all appearances, the ridge was far more assailable or less strongly occupied, because the Union troops seemed massed more with the view of repelling this projected assault toward their right.

Ewell says, try the Left.

Inasmuch as Ewell was really ignorant of what force was in his front at that moment, his advice to Lee may have sprung from a not unnatural desire to see that part of the army which had not been engaged do some of the work cut out for him and his corps.

Be that as it may, Lee then and there proposed giving up Gettysburg altogether, in order to draw Ewell over toward his right, thus massing the Confederate army in position to strike the Union left, as well as materially shortening his own long line.

But to this proposal Ewell as strongly demurred again. After losing over three thousand men in taking it, he did not want to give up Gettysburg. It involved a point of honor to which Jackson's successor showed himself keenly sensitive. His arrival had decided the day; and at that moment he held the bulk of the Union

What, give up Gettysburg.

army before him, simply by remaining where he was. If he moved off, that force would be freed also. So where would be the gain of it?

"Well, then, if I attack from my right, Longstreet will have to make the attack," said Lee at last; adding a moment later, and as if the admission came from him in spite of himself, "but he is so slow."

Finding that Ewell was averse to making an attack himself, averse to leaving Gettysburg; that Hill was averse to putting his crippled corps forward so soon again; and that Longstreet was averse to fighting at all on that ground,—Lee may Lee's   well have thought, like Napoleon dur-
Dilemma.   ing the Hundred Days, that his generals were no longer what they had been.[10] There was certainly more or less pulling at cross purposes in the Confederate camp.

Meade did not reach the field until one in the morning. It was then too early to see the ground he was going to fight on.

It thus appears that Lee had well considered all his plans for attacking before Meade could so much as begin his dispositions for defence. And this same unpreparedness, this fatality of having always to follow your adversary's lead, had so far distinguished every stage of this most unpromising campaign.

In the mellow moonlight of a midsummer's night, looking down into the unlighted streets of Gettysburg, the tired soldiers dropped to rest among the graves or in the fields wet with falling dew, while their comrades were hurrying on over the dusty roads that stretched out in long, weary miles toward Gettysburg, as if life and death were in their speed.

[1] It seems plain that next to Reynolds Hancock was the one in whom Meade reposed most confidence.

[2] This was the Seventh Indiana, which had been acting as escort to the trains. It brought five hundred fresh men to Wadsworth's division.

[3] By General Morgan's account, one thousand five hundred fugitives were collected by the provost guard of the Twelfth Corps, some miles in rear of the field.

[4] This was a brigade of nine months' men, called in derision the "Paper Collar Brigade." No troops contributed more to the winning of this battle, though only three of its five regiments were engaged.

[5] Johnson was then coming up. This is equivalent to an admission that Ewell did not feel able to undertake anything further that night with the two divisions that had been in action.

[6] While conveying the idea that the position was good, Hancock's message was, in reality, sufficiently ambiguous. It, however, served Meade's turn, as his mind was more than half made up already.

⁷ The Seventh Indiana brought up five hundred men; Stannard's brigade two thousand five hundred more.

⁸ The Union corps would not average ten thousand men present in the ranks, although the Sixth bore sixteen thousand on its muster rolls. Some corps had three, some two divisions. There were too many corps, and in consequence too many corps commanders, for the best and most efficient organization.

⁹ This was Pickett's, left at Chambersburg to guard the trains.

¹⁰ Lee's corps commanders in council seem more like a debating society: Meade's more like a Quaker meeting.

VII

THE SECOND OF JULY

W ith similar views each of the other's strength or weakness, Meade and Lee seem to have arrived at precisely the same idea. For instance, we have Lee seriously thinking of giving up Gettysburg, after hearing Ewell's objections to attacking from this side; and we have Meade first meditating a stroke against Lee from this very quarter, until dissuaded from it by some of his generals. Yet no sooner has Lee turned his attention to the other flank, than, as if informed of what was passing in his adversary's mind, Meade sets about strengthening that flank too. Wary and circumspect, each was feeling for his adversary's weak point.

Deliberating.

With the first streak of day the hostile camps were astir. Meade was riding along the ridge, giving orders for posting his troops. All of the

Twelfth Corps (Geary's division having vacated the position it had held during the night) planted itself still more firmly on the slopes of Culp's Hill, at the extreme right of the line. Wadsworth's division of the First Corps carried the line across the dip toward Cemetery Hill, where the Eleventh Corps had stood since the afternoon before. The Second Corps now fell in along the ridge, at the left of the Eleventh, resting its right on Ziegler's Grove, a little clump of trees hardly worth the name, growing out at the edge of the ridge, and where it bulges out somewhat brokenly. Next to the Second, the Third Corps lay massed behind the ridge, awaiting orders; it now held the left. The First was in reserve. The Fifth and Sixth were nearing the ground, but the pace was telling on the men.

Little Round Top deserted.

Union Line, Morning.

Since this day's battle was to be fought mostly on ground lying to the left (or south) of Hancock's position, it may be well to glance at its general features.

Three roads leave Gettysburg by way of Cemetery Hill, for Baltimore, Taneytown, and Emmetts-

burg, respectively. Those going to Baltimore and
Left Flank Emmettsburg part just as they begin to
Features. mount the slope of Cemetery Hill, the
first keeping off to the left over the hill, past the
Cemetery, and down the opposite slope, or wholly
within the Union lines; the last bearing off to the
right, along the foot of the hill, or wholly outside
Emmettsburg the Union lines, though at first within
Road. musket range. All of the Union army,
now assembled, lay between these two roads except that part posted at the east of the Cemetery
and along Culp's Hill. As for these troops, the
Baltimore Baltimore pike passed close by their
Turnpike. rear, the line here taking such a sharp
backward sweep that the soldiers posted on Culp's
Hill actually turned their backs on those forming
the front line. While the Baltimore pike cut the
Union position in two, or nearly so, the Taneytown road traversed it from end to end, thus
greatly facilitating the moving of troops or guns
from one part of the line to the other.

Though the Emmettsburg road closely hugged
the Cemetery Heights in going out of Gettysburg,
its general direction carried it farther and farther

off, in proportion as it went on its way; so that, although actually starting from Cemetery Hill, this road, in going two or three miles, eventually struck across to Seminary Ridge, or from the Union right to the enemy's right.[1] On the morning of the second it therefore formed debatable ground belonging to neither army, though offering a hazardous way still to belated troops, because the enemy had not yet occupied it. This Emmettsburg road was destined to play an important part in the events of this day.

After keeping its high level for some distance, Cemetery Ridge falls away for the space of several hundred yards, to rise again by a gradual slope to a rugged, bowlder-strewn, rather thinly wooded hill, called Little Round Top, which finely overlooks all that part of the field. Thus, what Culp's Hill was to the right Little Round Top was to the left of the Union position—at once bulwark and warder. Still beyond Little Round Top, out across a little valley opening a passage between them, rose a much loftier eminence, called Big Round Top. Strangely enough, neither

Little Round Top. See Chap. I.

Big Round Top.

of these commanding hills was occupied in the morning; for though Geary's pickets lay out before Little Round Top all night, they had been called in at daybreak, when the division itself marched off to rejoin its corps at Culp's Hill.[2] Most unfortunately, too, the Union cavalry was no longer there to watch the enemy's movements in this quarter and promptly report them at head-

Cavalry gone. quarters, as Meade himself had sent off Buford to the rear of the army.[3] In military phrase, the whole Union left was in the air.

Up to nine in the morning, therefore, this part of the field where Lee designed to strike his most telling blow viras anybody's position, so far as the dispositions for its defence are concerned; but at that hour Sickles[4] began deploying the Third Corps toward Round Top. Presently two of his brigades that had been left behind were seen marching down the Emmettsburg road, under fire from the enemy's skirmishers;[5] so giving them sharp notice that this road was no longer open.

Little Round Top, however, still remained

unoccupied, save by a handful of men belonging to the Signal Corps of the army.

The men of the Third Corps watched the march of their comrades in breathless expectation of hearing the enemy's cannon open upon them, or of seeing some body of infantry suddenly pour

Dangerous Marching.
a withering volley into them from the cover of the woods. But whether the enemy were too much confounded by the very audacity of the thing, or purposely refrained from hostilities that might expose and frustrate their own movements, now in progress under the mask of these very woods, neither of these things happened. These two lost brigades of Kearney's Peninsula veterans simply closed up their ranks, and strode steadily on between the two armies, without quickening their pace. In vain Sickles looked round him for some cavalry to escort them into his lines. There was no longer a single sabre on the ground.

Those of Sickles' soldiers who had thrown themselves down upon the grass behind the stacks now breathed more freely at seeing their comrades turn off from the main road, at a short mile out, where the roofs of a farmhouse and out-buildings glistened in the morning sun. This was the Sherfy place—a very paradise in appearance to these fasting and footsore soldiers, to whom its ripening fruits and luxuriant golden wheat, tall and nearly ripe for the sickle, seemed the incarnation of peace and plenty. Many a wistful glance was cast at the peach orchard, as these troops turned the corner where it stood. The cross-road then came straight down toward Little Round Top, so that in a quarter of an hour more the marching column heard the welcome orders to "Halt!" "Stack arms!" "Rest!"

Sherfy Place.

The Cross-road.

If the comparison be not too far-fetched, this Sherfy farm and the angle formed by these two divergent roads were destined to be the La Haie Sainte of this Waterloo. One word more is essential to the description. The ground out there, over which the cross-road passed on toward the Union lines, swells handsomely up to a rounded knoll that makes a very pretty as well as noticeable object in the landscape. The field-glasses of General Lee and of

The Enemy covet it.

his staff had already determined this knoll to be a splendid position for their artillery.

That peach-orchard angle with the adjoining knoll—in reality the highest point lying between the two armies—was, for this reason, the first object of the Confederates' attention on this day. It was a stepping-stone toward Cemetery Ridge. It was now in possession of Sickles' skirmishers, posted there the night before, and already exchanging shots with those of the enemy.[6]

Uneasy at seeing no enemy in front of him, Sickles decided to push his skirmishers still farther out. They accordingly went forward into the woods of Seminary Ridge, where the enemy was supposed to be. They had scarcely arrived there when they fell in with some Confederates, by whom, after a sharp encounter, they were driven back, but not before they had seen heavy columns moving off to gain the Union left under cover of the woods. This information made Sickles still more uneasy, impressed as he was with the belief that an attack upon him was imminent, and that he would have to receive it where the low ground he then occupied [7] offered little chance for mak-

ing a successful defence. Little Round Top rose
on his left, his front stretched across the adjoining
hollow, the peach-orchard knoll loomed threaten-
ingly before him in the distance, the skirmish fire

The Swale   was growing hotter out there, his or-
again.   ders were either vague or unsatisfac-
tory, and so Sickles, commanding a single corps
of the army, having convinced himself that the
line, as formed, was defective, determined in his
own mind to abandon it for one of his own choosing, orders or no orders.

This movement to the left, first detected by
Sickles' skirmishers, was Longstreet getting into
position for the attack that Lee had ordered.
When Longstreet's guns should be heard, Ewell

Longstreet   was to assault Culp's Hill and Cemetery
at Work.   Hill; while Hill, in the centre, was to
follow up Longstreet's attack as it progressed from
right to left. In short, a simultaneous assault on
the two wings of Meade's army was to be connected by a second and cumulative wave gathering headway as it rolled on, until this billow of
fire and steel should engulf and sweep the whole
Union line out of existence.

By this plan of battle Lee expected to discon-
cert any attempt to reinforce either flank, or
should Meade dare weaken his centre for that
purpose, Hill could then push in there, and cut
the Union army in twain.

Splendid conception! magnificent plan! none
the less because too complicated for the execution
of generals who either could not or would not
comprehend what was required of them. Con-
soling thought, that not all the stupidity or blun-
dering was on the Union side!

Lee had pointed out the peach orchard to
Longstreet, with the injunction that it should be
seized first of all.

Though he had received his orders at eleven
o'clock, it was not until after half-past three
that Longstreet was ready to open the battle.

3.30 P.M.   Sluggish by nature, he was well described by his chief as slow to act:
once in the thick of the fight, he rose with commanding power as the peerless fighter of that army;
and in that part of the field where Longstreet
fought, the dead always lay thickest. The confidence reposed in him by Lee is fully attested by

the fact of his having assigned the conduct of the battles, both on the second and third, to General Longstreet.

We have seen how, after some hours of wavering, Sickles had at length decided to choose a new position for himself. Yesterday he had not been able to convince himself that it would be right to move his corps out of line, even that he might go to the aid of his immediate chief and when his doing so would have saved the day. Restrained then by the strict letter of his orders, [8] he had remained in a state of feverish uncertainty for some hours, though at length concluding to disobey them. To-day when he was without real responsibility, being now in the presence of the general commanding the army, Sickles sets both orders and chief at defiance. The acts of the two days are, however, in striking accord. Sickles disobeys orders in both instances.

Sickles' Idea.

At about three o'clock the Union army saw with astonishment, not unmixed with dismay, the whole of the Third Corps moving out to the front in magnificent order, not as troops go into battle with skirmishers well advanced to the front, but as confidently as if going to a review with two grand armies for spectators. It was indeed a gallant sight to see these solid columns go forward, brigade after brigade, battery following battery, as, with flags fluttering in the breeze and bayonets flashing in the sun, the two divisions of Humphreys and Birney began deploying along the Emmettsburg road in front and taking position between the peach orchard and the Devil's Den to their rear, thus putting an elbow in the general line.

The Third Corps moves out.

In vain we try to imagine one of Napoleon's or Wellington's marshals taking it upon himself to post his troops independently of his commander. It now appears that General Sickles did this regardless of whether he was thwarting the plans of the general-in-chief or not, or whether indeed by so doing he was overthrowing the whole theory of delivering a strictly defensive battle. Instead of allowing Meade his initiative, we find Sickles actually compelling his superior to follow his lead,[9] not under the stress of some sudden emergency, but deliberately, defiantly. Not that he had penetrated Lee's designs. By no means. Had he done so we should be all the more amazed at his hardihood in going out with his ten thousand men to resist the onslaught of twenty thousand or more.

But the whole corps was not enough to occupy the ground selected. When the right division (Humphreys') reached the road, it had left a space of not less than three-fourths of a mile between itself and the left of the Second Corps. That flank was therefore in the air. The left division (Birney's), or most of it, was formed nearly at right angles with the first, showing a front of three brigades facing south, and posted in a line much broken by the natural features of the ground, which grow more and more rugged in proportion as Round Top is neared. Though stronger, by reason of the natural defences, this flank was a fourth of a mile from Round Top.

While this was going on out at the front, the Sixth and last Union Corps (Sedgwick's) was coming up behind the main position, worn down with marching thirty-six miles almost without a halt. The Fifth had already arrived, also with its men greatly fatigued. The situation, therefore, had so far improved, in that the enemy's delays [10] had given time for the whole Union army to assemble, though the two belated corps were scarcely in fighting trim.

Scarcely had Birney's men time to look about them when the booming of a single gun gave notice that the long-expected battle had begun.

[1] On the night of the first, the Confederate right did not extend much, if any, south of the Hagerstown, or Fairfield, road. As the fresh troops came up they were used in extending the line southward. Anderson's division was the first to move down to Hill's left. It was his skirmishers that first became engaged with Sickles'.

[2] We have seen Meade first planning an attack on that side, which was why he was drawing troops over there. He designed having the Third Corps occupy the position vacated by Geary, however, and so directed.

[3] In consequence of his exhausted condition, from incessant marching and fighting, Buford was to be relieved by other troops.

[4] General Daniel E. Sickles, commanding the Third Corps.

[5] The enemy were seeking to mask their movements to the Union left behind these skirmishers.

[6] The peach-orchard knoll was Sickles' bugbear. He thought it much to be preferred to the position he was in. It was, however, fully commanded from Little Round Top.

[7] This refers to the swale next north of Little Round Top.

[8] Though forming part of Reynolds' command, Sickles was halted between Taneytown and Emmettsburg by Meade's order.

[9] Sickles claimed at first that he could not find the position assigned him, namely, that vacated by Geary. The force of this plea will be best appreciated by old soldiers. But in the following remarks all such clumsy pretexts are thrown to the winds; he here takes praise to himself for ignoring his commanding officer. It might be called a plea for insubordination.

"It may have been imprudent to advance and hold Longstreet at whatever sacrifice, but wasn't it worth a sacrifice to save the key of the position? What were we there for? Were we there to count the cost in blood and men, when the key of the position at Gettysburg was within the enemy's grasp?" (How did Sickles know this?) "What little I know of conduct on a battlefield I learned from Hooker and Kearney." (Kearney was a strict disciplinarian.) "What would Hooker or Kearney have done, finding themselves in an assailable, untenable position, without orders from headquarters as to their dispositions for battle, when they saw masses of the enemy marching to seize a vital point? Would they have hesitated? Would they have sent couriers to headquarters and asked for instructions what to do? Never, never! Well, I learned war from them, and I didn't send any. I simply advanced on to the battlefield and seized Longstreet by the throat and held him there."—*Sickles' Music Hall Speech, Boston, 1886.*

[10] John Stark's famous maxim, that one fresh man in battle is worth two fatigued ones, will be heartily endorsed by all who have seen it put to the test.

VIII

THE SECOND OF JULY — *Continued*

AT this signal all the enemy's batteries opened in succession, and for a space a storm of shot and shell tore through Sickles' lines with crushing effect. His own guns, posted partly in

Fighting begins.

the orchard, partly along the cross-road, on the high knoll behind it, — that is to say, in the very spot selected by Lee in advance for his own, — began to lose both horses and men, nor were the infantry able to shelter themselves from the cross-fire of fifty-four pieces of artillery, some of which were killing men at both sides of the angle with the same shot.[1]

Not many minutes had elapsed before every man on the ground, from general to private soldier, felt that a wretched blunder had been committed in thrusting them out there.

By and by the cannonade slackened. This was sufficient notice to old soldiers that something

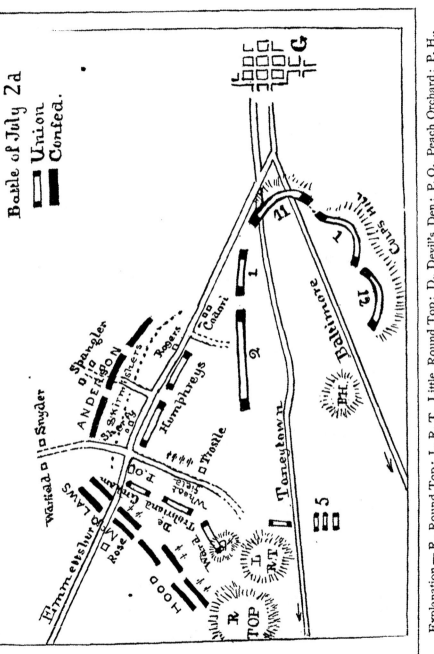

Battle of July 2d

Union ▭
Confed. ▬

Explanation — R, Round Top; L. R. T., Little Round Top; D, Devil's Den; P. O., Peach Orchard; P. H., Powers' Hill; G, Gettysburg.

more was coming. Before its echoes had died away
Longstreet's first assaulting column, led
by Hood himself, came down with a
crash upon Birney, three lines deep.

See his Troops
described,
p. 26.

The enemy was about to repeat his old tactics,
employed at Chancellorsville with so much effect,
of getting around the Union left and then rolling
it up endwise.[2] That his calculations in this case
were not quite accurate was soon made manifest.

Since noon Longstreet had been working his
way round through the woods toward Little
Round Top,   making a wide circuit to avoid discovery.[3] Having remonstrated in vain against
this movement, he was probably in no great hurry
to execute it. It was therefore four o'clock before
he was ready to begin. But if slow he was sure.

Longstreet's line crossed the Emmettsburg
road at an acute angle with it, Hood's division
stretching off to the right, McLaws' mostly to the
left. Longstreet was thus about to throw eight
brigades, or, by his own account, thirteen thousand
men, against the three brigades of Ward, De Trobriand, and Graham, numbering about five thousand men. Hood was to begin by attacking from

the wheat-field to the Devil's Den, McLaws to follow him up from the wheat-field to the orchard. It was not until they had got into line, however, that the Confederates were undeceived about the Union force before them. Until then they thought the Union left stopped at the orchard.

At four o'clock the Union signal-station on Little Round Top saw and reported these movements to headquarters. The Confederate advance began soon after four. By the first fire Hood was wounded and had to leave the field almost before his troops had fairly come into action.

The first shock fell upon Ward's brigade, which held the extreme left at the Devil's Den. Ward's line would not reach to Little Round Top, so that there was a wide space between him and this hill, with not a man in it — a fact that Hood's men were

Combat at Devil's Den.

not slow either in perceiving or taking advantage of. But, what was far worse, it led to the discovery of the defenceless condition of Little Round Top itself, and, quickly grasping its commanding importance, the enemy instantly sent one of his brigades to seize it.

The conflict thus established at this point,

which Sickles had so imprudently vacated, became of supreme importance to the Union army, while that about to begin at the peach orchard degenerated into a struggle to save Sickles' corps from annihilation.

Fortunately for Ward, the ground he held was just the place for a protracted defence, provided he should not be out-flanked. Weird and grisly, it looked as if some huge excrescent mass of earth, rocks, and trees had some time slid off the flank of Little Round Top into the low ground below, whence its own momentum had carried it still farther on—a misshapen heap, deeply seamed by rents and splits, thick-set with bowlders and filled with holes and hiding-places, among which Ward's men now found excellent cover.

Ward was firmly planted on and around the Devil's Den, with his sharp-shooters loading and firing from behind the scattered bowlders, when the enemy made their rush upon him, whooping and yelling like so many fiends come to reoccupy The Danger their own legitimate abode. Some Point. portion soon found themselves in the unguarded hollow below. Seeing the enemy crowding into it, Ward sent first one regiment there, and then another, on the run. A combat at close quarters ensued.

The regiments of Hood's division were now either trying to scale Little Round Top, push through the hollow, or capture the Devil's Den with its guns. The left brigade, however, which extended beyond the Den, was being very roughly handled; the centre only had made progress, while the right was engaged in a murderous conflict, to be presently described. Hood's effort had, therefore, exhausted itself, and his division had to halt simply because it could advance no farther.

McLaws now came to Hood's assistance. His right brigade (Kershaw's) now struck De Trobriand's, which stood next in line along the edge of a wheat-field, back of and adjoining the Devil's Den. De Trobriand had a little muddy ravine in front of him, into which the enemy boldly plunged. His men waited until their assailants had got within twenty yards, when they poured in such a close and deadly fire that the gully was speedily vacated by all save the dead and the dying. The attack here not

At the Wheat-field.

only completely failed, but three of Kershaw's regiments were nearly destroyed while attacking the peach orchard. This brigade fell back and was rallied about the Rose house.

Semmes' brigade had followed close behind Kershaw's, and now took its place. Its commander speedily fell, mortally wounded. Barksdale rushed upon Graham, followed by Wofford. This onset brought the whole Confederate force into action. The odds were as two to one.

That part of the enemy whom we left working their way up the hollow to Little Round Top also met with stubborn resistance, and as this was more and more seen to be the critical point, the enemy redoubled their efforts to force their way through. Our soldiers who had gone into ambuscade behind the bowlders there were being gradually driven back from cover to cover, so yielding up as they retired the approaches to Little Round Top.

Having gained this vantage-ground the Confederates now made a second onset against Ward and De Trobriand. This time it proved more successful. After an hour's obstinate fighting,

Ward was driven out of his fastness,[4] De Tro-
Devil's Den briand forced back across the wheat-
taken. field. Sickles' left was thus completely
broken up, the fragments drifting backward in
search of some point of support.

Little Round Top was about to fall into the
enemy's hands. Once in his possession, the
Union line on Cemetery Ridge would have to be
abandoned or swept to the winds. Fortunately
the turning-point had been reached before the
rebels could reap the reward of Ward's repulse.
Little Round Shortly before Hood's onset began,
Top in Peril. General Warren, of the Engineers, had
seen from his signal-station on Little Round Top
the enemy's line advancing to the attack. In one
moment his experienced eye took in all the
danger. Ordering the signal officers to keep on
waving their flags, Warren first sent for and then
dashed off in search of assistance himself. Indeed, not a moment was to be lost. By a fortunate
chance some troops were met moving out to reinforce Sickles. Detaching a regiment, Warren
hurried it off to the threatened point. Meantime,
in response to his request, though without his

knowing it, Vincent's brigade was climbing the rearmost slopes off Little Round Top, arriving just in time to save the hill with the bayonet.[5]

A murderous hand-to-hand conflict now began among the rocks and trees, with those of the enemy who were trying to scale the slopes regardless of death or wounds. Sometimes the assailants were firing at each other from behind the same bowlder; sometimes both fell at the same instant. The strife was still unequal. A battery was dragged to the summit; [6] three of the cannoneers were shot in succession before the fourth succeeded in firing off the piece. Another regiment was brought up. The rebels fought as if determined to take that hill or die: the Union soldiers as if they had made up their minds to perish to the last man in its defence. On both sides men fell fast, the bravest first of all. Vincent was killed outright, Weed mortally wounded, and only a moment later Hazlett, who had so gallantly scaled with his guns slopes seemingly inaccessible, was struck down while in the act of stooping over his commander's prostrate body. O'Rorke was killed while encouraging his men. All the superior officers were down. Never were rifles wielded by such deadly marksmen as those Texans of Hood's!

Finding all their efforts to carry the hill by storm useless, the rebels next made a rush up through the little valley separating the two Round Tops, with the view of taking the defenders in the rear. The 20th Maine met this assault. "Stand firm, men!" was the command. As if maddened to desperation, the enemy flung themselves upon the hardy backwoodsmen from the Pine Tree State. Twice they were forced backward over the crest, and twice they rallied and drove their assailants back in their turn. But the emergency had now been perceived and was being provided for. Fresh troops dashed over the hill to the aid of those who were fighting. A final charge sent the rebels reeling down into the hollow, and out of it. by the way they came, leaving five hundred prisoners in the hands of the defenders, through whose gallantry the danger, though perilously imminent, had been averted.

Little Round Top saved.

Meantime the peach orchard was being furi-

ously attacked. Exposed here to a severe cross-
fire, the Union line crumbled away
at every discharge. The resistance was
stubborn, as might be expected from such good
soldiers as Graham's, but even they could not
long maintain such a disadvantageous position,
and though the attacking brigades were badly cut
up, the enemy broke through there after a bloody
contest. Barksdale swept on over the guns,
Wofford gathered up what he left behind. All
that men could do to stem the tide was done, and
all in vain. Graham was wounded and
taken prisoner, Sickles himself carried
off the field, shot thrsough the leg. In less than
two hours Birney's line was clean gone.

McLaws assaults.

Sickles wounded.

As the infantry fell back from the orchard, the
artillery posted along the cross-road behind them
became, of course, the enemy's object. Many of
these guns had to be abandoned, some sacrificed in
the effort to delay the enemy's progress. Bige-
low's battery obeyed the order to fight to the last
with a constancy as worthy of lasting commemora-
tion as Perry's famous "Don't give up the ship!"

Though the position itself was scarcely worth

the sacrifice of a single soldier, it was felt that Sickles' troops must be extricated at any cost; and since a battle had been forced we must not be the losers.

So after sending Vincent's brigade to Little Round Top, the rest of Barnes' division went out to help maintain the line where De Trobriand had been fighting; and Caldwell's division of the Second Corps also went to Ward's assistance.

Efforts to help Sickles.

Repulsed from Little Round Top, the enemy fell upon Caldwell. The struggle was brief but bitter. Half a score of general and field officers went down on the Union side. But Caldwell finally succeeded in driving the enemy back across the ravine from which Ward had been dislodged, and two brigades of regulars firmly closed the gap toward Little Round Top.

But the point of support at the orchard being gone, all these troops were in turn driven back after repeated charges and countercharges made across the wheat-field had piled it with the slain of both armies.

Anderson's Confederate division now advanced

to perform its share of the work cut out for it; namely, of continuing the assault from right to left.

One side of the angle being swept away, being violently assaulted both in front and flank, Hum-

Humphreys driven off. phreys also had to fall back from the Emmettsburg road to the main position, or be cut off from it. Everything that had been fighting on Sickles' new line was now going to the rear in more or less confusion. The enemy were now masters of the whole of that line, had inflicted serious losses upon the Third and Fifth Corps, and had taken some of Sickles' guns. We had only Round Top to show for the terrible struggle resulting from Sickles' advance.

These disasters could not make our generals give up beaten yet. Crawford's" Pennsylvania Reserves," a splendid body of well-seasoned soldiers, were now ordered to drive the victorious enemy beyond the wheat-field. Seizing a color, the general himself led the charging column

Crumbs of Comfort. across this thrice-fought field, clearing it in the most gallant manner. Two brigades of the Sixth Corps followed this mosvement. These prompt measures completely discouraged all further efforts on the enemy's part in this quarter. Longstreet withdrew his shattered forces to the peach orchard. In these unavailing assaults he had lost upwards of five thousand men. Hood was wounded, Barksdale killed, and Semmes mortally wounded.[7]

After this repulse, some of Doubleday's division went out to the Emmettsburg road, capturing the enemy's post at the Rogers house on that road.

It was now growing dark. Lee's brilliant plan of consecutive attack from right to left had dwindled to a series of isolated combats—a blow here and a blow there, instead of those combined and telling strokes he had designed giving all along the Union line.[8]

In falling back upon Cemetery Ridge, which was done in admirable order, Humphreyss was followed up by three of Hill's brigades, one of which, Wright's, actually succeeded in reaching the crest, and had even seized some of the guns there, before troops could be brought up to check it. The other brigades having failed to support it, this one was

Cemetery Ridge pierced.

easily driven off, though its having pierced the Union centre with so little opposition undoubtedly led Lee to think the thing not so difficult, after all. We think it was the controlling motive for his attack on the third.

One other conflict remains to be noticed. The peril menacing his left had induced Meade to nearly strip Culp's Hill of its defenders. All of the Twelfth Corps, which, it will be remembered, held Culp's Hill and its approaches, had been hurried over to the left, except one brigade, thus abandoning the rude but substantial breastworks that these troops had raised with felled trees, earth, Culp's Hill or loose stones, against an attack. As deserted. yet all seemed quiet on this side; but when, shortly after sunset, Ewell's corps tardily began the part assigned it by pouring out of the woods in which it had lain concealed, to begin a furious assault upon Culp's Hill, his men found nothing before them except the undefended works just spoken of on that part of the hill bordering And is upon Rock Creek. Finding the door occupied. standing open, as it were, they had only to walk in and take possession.

Trifling as it seems when relating it, this was by far the most important, we might say the only real, advantage gained by the enemy in all this day's fighting, with its frightful losses in men and material—and for this reason: The point seized The Danger was within short musket-shot of the of it. Baltimore pike, and quite near that part of it where the reserve Union artillery was parked. This might be seized or stampeded. More than this, the pike led first to Westminster, where Meade had fixed his base of supplies before moving up to Gettysburg, so making it from necessity his line of retreat in case of a reverse to the army. In short, this was one of those desperate cases that admit only of desperate remedies; either the Confederates must be driven out before they could look about them, or the army must retreat. Again, night undoubtedly saved the Union army from a great disaster.

Farther to the left Greene's brigade met and repulsed every assault made upon them. The combat took place in the thick woods, already darkened by the approach of night.

While this was happening at Culp's Hill, the

rest of Early's Confederate division came on in the early twilight to the assault of Cemetery Hill. The day had worn itself out, the west only glowed a sullen red upon the battlefield. Early's dusky lines could scarce be made out except by the flashes of musketry seen here and there. One of his brigades struck the side nearest Culp's Hill (the gap side), where the Union infantry were kneeling behind stone walls, waiting with guns cocked for them to get up nearer; the other brigade, with a third in reserve, marched on the right of the first. Thirty odd guns flamed and thundered upon them from the Cemetery. The hillside was lighted up by flashes of musketry. It was one incessant blaze and roar. The left brigade was mowed down in swaths, and had to give way; but that on the right forced its way through the ranks of the infantry, swarmed up around the guns that were dealing death among them, and began a hand-to-hand fight with the artillery-men, in which men were beaten to death with handspikes and rammers.

The Confederates enjoyed a short-lived triumph.

Cemetery stormed.

An ominous silence succeeded the struggle around
Enemy is repulsed. the guns. Word was passed that the enemy was in our works. Orders were given in whispers, for it was now too dark to tell friend from foe. The steady tramp, tramp of armed men was now heard approaching. Presently, out of the darkness, a brigade of the Second Corps rushed in with a cheer. Being joined by other troops, all fell upon the exultant Confederates, who, finding themselves left without support, saved themselves as they could. As it was, not half of them got back to their own lines.

This ended the fighting for the day. Darkness and exhaustion summoned the weary soldiers of both armies to a much-needed rest. Thus far the two days' fighting had proved indecisive. On the left the enemy had taken a somewhat closer hold, yet the Union position was everywhere practically intact except at Culp's Hill.[9] It is true that both armies were much weakened from loss of blood, although their relative strength remained much as before. Perhaps the Union army had suffered most, because its reinforcements were thrown in piecemeal, and badly cut up before they could render effective assistance.

It now began to be understood that if the Union army had not sustained a defeat, it was not so much because of any natural strength of the ground, since the Confederates had twice forced a way to it, as because its form enabled troops to concentrate upon the threatened point with great rapidity. To lengthen it out, as Sickles had done, was to throw away this advantage. He had finally been forced to retake his natural position. Herein, we think, lies the whole secret of Meade's successful defence. The first of July was an accident: the second, a blunder.

[1] The two roads, Emmettsburg and cross-road, lay on converging ridges, which formed the angle at the orchard. It was a very irregular line, however, running first round the orchard, then along a ravine at the edge of the wheat-field to the Devil's Den, and again across this to the hollow, where it swung back so as to embrace the Den.

[2] Lee's order of battle had been made in the belief that by throwing Longstreet across the Emmettsburg road he would envelop the Union army's proper left, whereas we have seen that he was wholly at fault, until Sickles made a condition where it did not exist before.

[3] In their effort to keep out of sight the enemy lost two hours. Two hours sooner they would have occupied the orchard without hinderance.

[4] The enemy took three guns here that could not be got off.

⁵ Vincent's and Weed's brigades of the Fifth Corps were thrown upon Little Round Top in succession, each regiment going in under fire.

⁶ "The battery went up that rocky hill, through the woods on the east side, at a trot, with spurs and whips vigorously applied. I do not believe a piece barked a tree . . . we went there at a trot,each man and horse trying to pull the whole battery by hismself."—*Licut.* *Ritten- house.*

⁷ Kershaw and Semmes were both driven back to the Rose house, the former losing over six hundred men, the latter being killed; but Barksdale, supported by Wofford, bore down all opposition, thus allowing the defeated brigades to rally and come up again.

⁸ The whole history of this day shows that Hill's corps had been too badly hurt on the first to take any efficient part on the second. Practi- cally Longstreet was left to fight it out alone.

⁹ At the close of the day the enemy held, on the left, the base of the Round Tops, Devil's Den, its woods, and the Emmettsburg road; on the right he had effected a lodgement at Culp's Hill.

IX

THE THIRD OF JULY

THE events of the second seem to have impressed the two generals quite differently. In Lee the combative spirit rose even higher. To Meade the result seemed, on the whole, discouraging. The enemy held a strong vantage-ground on his right; his line had been twice pierced. Would he be better able to hold it now that the army was weakened by the loss of eight to ten thousand men?

At nightfall a council of war was called, and the situation discussed. Meade desired to know first the condition of the troops, and next the temper of his officers. To this end they were separately asked whether they favored a removal of the Meade's army to some other position, or waiting Council. another attack where they now were. The general voice was in favor of fighting it out to the bitter end, and it was so determined.

A strong force of infantry and artillery was therefore moved over to the right, in readiness to expel the enemy there at break of day.

Deeming the result of the day's operations to be on the whole favorable to him, Lee was equally determined to fight to a finish. As Napoleon had said before him, in a similar spirit of impulsive ex-

Lee not beaten yet.

ultation, when satisfied that Wellington was awaiting his onslaught at Waterloo, "I have them now, those English!" so Lee now replied to all Longstreet's remonstrances by shaking his clenched fist at Cemetery Hill, exclaiming as he did so, "The enemy is there, and I am going to strike him!"

He too, therefore, strongly reinforced his left at Culp's Hill, with the view of having a heavy force well in hand there, ready to strike in upon the Union right and rear, while a formidable column of wholly fresh troops, charging it in the centre, should cut that in two, seize the Baltimore pike, and with Ewell's help crush everything on that side. In order to reap to the utmost the advan-

Plan of Attack.

tages looked for as certain, Stuart's cavalry, now back with the army, was sent far round to the Union rear, with orders to strike the Baltimore pike as soon as the retreat should begin.

To guard against some such movement, or in fact any demonstration towards its rear, the Union cavalry was posted on this pike, a few miles back of Cemetery Ridge. Still another cavalry force was guarding the Union left, beyond Round Top.

These dispositions present, in brief, the preparations both generals were making for the third day's conflict.

Lee had silenced Longstreet's objections by ordering him to get ready Pickett's fresh division for the decisive charge on Cemetery Ridge. These soldiers, Virginians all, bitterly complained be- Pickett to cause they were only the rear-guard of lead it. that army which they were told was driving the Yankees before them in utter rout. Their charge was to be preceded and sustained by turning every gun in the Confederate army upon the point of attack.

With the first streak of day the struggle for the possession of Culp's Hill began again. As both sides had orders to attack, there was no delay in

commencing. Soon from every commanding spot
the Union batteries were sending their shot crash-
ing and tearing through the woods in which the
Confederates lay hid, smiting the forest with a
tempest of iron, throwing down branches, and
plowing up the earth in great furrows.[1] Stirred
up by this shower of missiles, Ewell's men poured
forth from the valley of Rock Creek, and rushed
up the hillside in front, to begin anew the sanguinary struggle they had only ceased from on
the previous night. Here among the gray rocks
and aged oaks—the pleasure-ground, in fact, of
the people of Gettysburg—a contest raged for
hours, similar to that which Little Round Top
had witnessed on the previous afternoon.

One piece of hopeless heroism deserves com-
memoration in all accounts of this battle. In the
height of the engagement an order was brought
for two regiments, the Second Massachusetts and
the Twenty-seventh Indiana, to charge across the
meadow stretching between Culp's Hill and Mc-
Allister's Hill, on the other side of which the enemy lay in the old intrenchments. To try to pass
that meadow was rushing to certain destruction.

"Are you sure that is the order?" was demanded of the officer who brought it. "Positive," was the reply. "Up, men—fix bayonets—forward!" was the ringing command. One regiment reached the works, the other faltered midway under the terrible fire. As many were lost in falling back as in going forward. Only half the men got back to the lines unhurt.

After seven hours of this kind of fighting, the assailants were finally driven beyond Rock Creek again, leaving five hundred prisoners, besides their Culp's Hill dead and wounded, behind them. Again retaken. an essential part of Lee's plan of attack had signally failed, and once more the whole Union line stretched unbroken from Culp's Hill to Round Top.

But it was only eleven o'clock; and though the battle had gone against him on this side, Lee seems to have felt, like Desaix at Marengo, that there was still time to gain another. Was it here that Lee lost that moral equipoise which seems born in really great commanders in moments of supreme peril?

Be that as it may, the order was given for his

artillery to open. Longstreet had massed seventy-five guns in one battery, Hill sixty-three, and Ewell enough more to bring the number up to one hundred and fifty in all. At precisely one

The Cannon-ade. o'clock the signal guns were fired. Before their echoes died away the whole line of Confederate batteries was blazing like a volcano. There seemed to be but one flash and one report, and their simultaneous discharges, pealing out deafening salvos, went rolling and rolling on through the valleys, and echoing among the hills, in one mighty volume of sound, vying with the loudest thunder. It was sub-limely grand, sublimely terrifying. Without a moment's warning, as if the heavens above had opened and the earth below yawned beneath their feet, the Union soldiers found themselves in the midst of the pitiless storm. A tornado of shot and shell burst upon Cemetery Hill, tearing the air, rending the rocks, plowing up the ground, and dealing death on all sides at once.

This terrific cannonade, under which the solid earth shook, the sky was darkened at noonday, the valley filled with thick-rolling smoke, the air with explosions and nameless rubbish, and which seemed announcing the coming of the Last Day, is thus described by an eye-witness:—

"The storm broke upon us so suddenly that soldiers and officers who leaped, as it began, from their tents, or from lazy siestas on the grass, were stricken at their rising with mortal wounds, and died, some with cigars between their lips, some with pieces of food in their fingers, and one at least—a pale young German from Pennsylvania —with a miniature of his sister in his hands. Horses fell shrieking out such awful cries as Cooper told of, and writhing themselves about in hopeless agony. The boards of fences, scattered by explosions, flew in splinters through the air. The earth, torn up in clouds, blinded the eyes of hurrying men; and through the branches of the trees and among the gravestones of the cemetery a shower of destruction crashed ceaselessly. The hill, which seemed alone devoted to this rain of death, was clear in nearly all its unsheltered places within five minutes after the fire began."

Eighty guns replied from the Union position

almost as soon, so that the very air between the two armies was alive with flying missiles.[2] During the cannonade the Union infantry were lying down in open ranks behind the crest, taking it, for the most part, with remarkable steadiness. As the enemy's artillerists mostly overshot the ridge, the ground behind was a place of even greater danger. The little farmhouse standing on the Taneytown road, occupied as army headquarters, was so riddled that the general was compelled to seek a safer spot. Even as far back as Culp's Hill, where the Twelfth Corps were still facing their assailants, the enemy's shot came plunging and plowing through the ranks from behind, thus killing men by a fire in the rear.

After this indescribable uproar had lasted upwards of two hours, the Union batteries were ordered to cease firing in order to husband their ammunition for what every man in the army knew was coming.

It was now three o'clock. The moment had come for the supreme effort of all.

All the Union generals now set themselves to work repairing the damages caused by the cannonade—re-forming ranks, replacing dismantled guns, rectifying positions, exhorting the men to stand firm, and, in short, themselves offering the highest examples of coolness and soldierly conduct.

We had a first line of infantry posted along the foot of the heights,—some behind stone walls, when these followed the natural line of defence, as they now and then did; some behind rocky inequalities of the ground,—with artillery above and Union behind it; and there was a second line Defences. of infantry back of the crest. Although Meade is said to have expected, and even told some of his officers, that Lee's next blow would fall on the Union centre, we detect no specific preparation to meet it.

The troops designated for the assault were waiting only for the order to advance, Pickett's splendid division on the right, Pettigrew's, lately Heth's, on the left, with two brigades in support of Pickett, two in support of Pettigrew, and still another marching at some distance in the rear. The Storming Though the equals of any in that army, Column. Heth's soldiers had been so much shaken by their encounter with the First Corps that they were far from showing the same ardor as Pickett's men. All told, the assaulting force numbered not less than fifteen thousand, and probably more.[3]

Pickett was watching the effect of the artillery-fire when a courier brought him word from the batteries that if he was coming at all now was his time, as the Union guns had slackened their fire. After reading it himself, Pickett handed the note to Longstreet at his side. "General, shall I advance?" Pickett asked his chief. Mastered by his emotions, Longstreet could only give a nod of assent and turn away. "I shall lead my division forward, sir," was the soldierly reply.

As the charging column passed through them to the front, fifteen or eighteen guns followed close behind in support.

Friend and foe alike have borne testimony to the steadiness with which this gallant band met the ordeal — by much the hardest that falls to the soldier's lot — of having to endure a terrible fire without the power of returning it. No sooner had the long gray lines come within range than the Union artillery opened upon it, right and left. For a quarter of an hour the march was kept up in the face of a storm of missiles. Cemetery Hill was lighted up by the flashes. Little Round Top struck in sharply. Smoke and flame burst from the batteries along Cemetery Ridge. Solid shot tore through the ranks; shells were bursting under their feet, over their heads, in their faces; men, or the fragments of men, were being tossed in the air every moment, but, closing up the gaps and leaving swaths of dead and dying in their track, these men kept up their steady march to the front, as if conscious that the eyes of both armies were upon them. They had been told that the enemy's artillery was silenced!

As soon as they could do so without injury to their own men, the Confederate guns began afresh, Pickett's so that again shells streamed through Advance. the air and balls bounded over the plain without intermission, dense smoke shutting out the assailants from view.

Protected by the fire of this redoubtable artillery, the column continued its deliberate march. When within five hundred yards, or about to cross the Emmettsburg road, it suddenly moved off by the left flank a short distance, as if to close up a break in the line or recover the true point of attack — some say one and some say the other. Be that as it may, Pickett's men first received the fire of Stannard's Vermont brigade while making this flank march, and again encountered it on their flank after facing to the front for the purpose of resuming their advance toward the heights.

This must be considered, we think, as the turning-point in the assault. Stannard's attack, made at such close quarters, so shattered Pickett's right brigade that this flank of the assaulting column never reached the crest at all, but drifted more and more to the rear, lost to all organization. Thus was repeated that memorable manœuvre of the Fifty-second Regiment against the Imperial Guard at Waterloo, and with like results; for before the close and deadly fire poured in upon them at only a few rods' distance — a fire they were powerless to return — Pickett's right was either shot to pieces or crowded in upon the centre, so throwing it into disorder and checking its momentum, while tne Green Mountain boys, aided now by other troops, clung to their mutilated flank, following it up step by step, and firing into it as fast as the men could load.

Eight batteries were now pouring canister into Pickett at point-blank range, carrying away whole ranks of men at every discharge. Before him, between two little clumps of trees, which Lee himself had carefully pointed out and Pickett was making such heroic efforts to reach, lay the Second Union Corps. As the men of this corps realized that the brunt of the charge was to fall on them, they grew restive and anxious; but Gibbon, curbing their impatience with voice and gesture, quietly said, as he passed along the ranks, "Hold your fire, boys — they are not near enough yet."

Pickett's first line had come within a hundred and fifty yards when the order was given to fire. It was followed by a terrible volley before which that line went down like grass before the scythe. When the smoke rolled away the charging lines were seen inextricably mixed together, all order lost — a frantic mob covered with blood and dirt,

with scarce a general officer left, but not in retreat.
On the contrary, with a rush and a roar, heard
above the din of cannon and musketry, the surging mass came rolling and tumbling on, like waves
The Final   against a rocky shore, firing, screeching,
Charge.   brandishing swords and battle-flags, one
moment swallowed up in smoke, the next emerg-

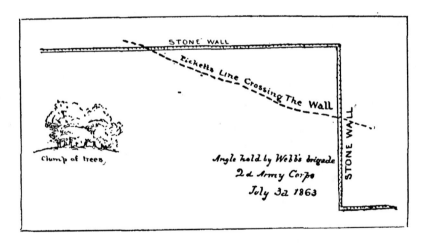

Point where Pickett's Charge was stopped.

ing a few paces nearer. Officers became separated
from their men; generals no longer led their own
brigades, but with uplifted swords rushed on to the
front, calling on their men to follow. One after
another they fall. Individual example and heroism

were the only things that could count here, and neither was wanting. One thought and one purpose seemed to animate them, and that was that they must either conquer or die. Sublime heroism! Sublime folly!

In this manner one portion of the Confederates struck and overwhelmed the first Union line, driving its defenders back upon the second. Here they turned and faced their infuriated assailants, who, led on by Armistead, had leaped the last stone wall, shooting down or bayoneting all those found crouching behind it, had then rushed up to seize the solitary gun that had just fired its last shot in their faces, and, as if victory was assured, already had raised their cry of triumph on the disputed summit.

Though divided and thrown off by this entering wedge, the Union soldiers, who now came swaying up from right to left, soon seized it as in a vise. For a few minutes an indescribable mêlée raged here on half an acre of ground, at push of bayonet, hand to hand, muzzle to muzzle, breast to

The Repulse. breast. Gradually the enclosing lines surged forward. Armistead was shot down by the side of the captured gun. The Confederates turned to fly, but found the way barred to them on every side. Imbedded by its own force, the living wedge could not be withdrawn. They surrendered in swarms, while those who dared the dangers of again crossing that fatal plain, now spread themselves out over it in every direction.

When it was all over with Pickett, the two supporting brigades came up on the right, only to be repulsed by a few volleys. Pettigrew had been defeated almost before he could come to close quarters, Pickett destroyed, Wilcox brushed away.

From his post of observation Longstreet had watched the advance up the ridge. "I saw," he says, "the crest of the hill lit up with a solid sheet of flame. When the smoke cleared away the division was gone. Nearly two-thirds lay dead on the field, and the survivors were sullenly retreating down the hill. Mortal man could not have stood that fire."

Again the old story. An assaulting column has been driven through an opposing line, it is true, but with the loss of all organization, without a supporting force to follow up the advantage it has gained, it finds itself in a trap where it is in danger of being sacrificed to the last man. Unable to execute the simplest manœuvre, it is at the mercy of any organized body brought against it. Lee seemed to have forgotten Fredericksburg. Longstreet did better at Chickamauga.

Two cavalry battles belong to the complete history of this remarkable day, though in no way affecting the main result. In the first Stuart attacked and was defeated. This was Cavalry Battles. cavalry against cavalry; and as Pickett's front attack was repulsed, that in the rear amounted to little in itself. In the second Kilpatrick made a bold dash into Hood's rear, about Round Top, with the view of throwing the enemy into confusion, breaking up his line there, and so facilitating an advance by the Union forces in that quarter. This was cavalry against infantry in position, and the ground the worst possible for cavalry manœuvres. For an hour the enemy had our troopers riding round them with drawn sabres, receiving the fire first of one regiment and then of another. No advantage being taken of the diversion, the cavalry was nearly cut to pieces.

¹ To this day the woods show the destructive effects of this cannonade.

² "I instructed the chiefs of artillery and battery commanders to withhold their fire for fifteen or twenty minutes after the cannonade commenced, then to concentrate their fire with all possible accuracy upon those batteries which were most destructive to us, but slowly, so that when the enemy's ammunition was exhausted we should have enough left to meet the assault." — *Gen. Hunt, Chief of Artillery.*

³ Pickett's division with two brigades absent was probably five thousand five hundred strong, Heth's not less, and the three supporting brigades as many more. The troops were no doubt selected as the very best that offered.

X

THE RETREAT

THRICE had the sun gone down on that ensanguined field, where one hundred and fifty thousand men had striven for the mastery and forty thousand sealed their devotion with their blood. Exhausted by their efforts, the Confederates thought only of making good their retreat. Gettysburg was immediately evacuated and both wings drawn back on the main body, so that, as now re-formed and contracted, Lee's army stretched from Oak Hill to the peach orchard. Behind this line, and under cover of its woods, he was now getting ready to retreat.

Gettysburg evacuated.

Lee's New Position.

Such plain indications could hardly be overlooked.[1] A reconnoisance from the Union left found the Confederates retiring. During the night the Union troops went forward to the battlefield of the 2d.

Lee's lost opportunity on the 1st was as nothing to Meade's on the 3d. It came when the Confederates were in the confusion resulting from their repulse. It was lost, however, because the great captain was not there.

Lost Chances. Meade was unequal to exacting a supreme effort at this moment, either from his army or himself. To let slip this opportunity was to tempt fortune itself, and it never came again.

But if from any of the many causes alleged,[2] or all of them put together, the one chance out of a thousand, for which all this marching and fighting had been going on, had eluded Meade's grasp, or if it be conceded that he found Lee's new position so strong as to hold out no hope of a successful assault, history will still demand to know why this beaten army, short of ammunition, encumbered with its wounded, its prisoners, and its wagons, thirty to forty miles from the Potomac, with a mountain defile to pass and a

Strange Inaction. wide river to cross, was suffered to march off unmolested with all its immense spoil, and not only to do that, but to remain eleven days between Gettysburg and the Potomac without being once seriously attacked.

That Lee could not long remain on Seminary Ridge, let his position be ever so strong, was a self-evident proposition. He had exhausted his means of attack, his army was cut down by more than twenty thousand men, his ammunition was nearly expended, nor could it be replenished short of Virginia. His means of defence were therefore extremely limited. If it had been possible to detain Lee where he was, even for a few days longer, his surrender was a foregone conclusion without firing another shot. But taking the situation as we find it, we do not see how he could have been more critically placed, if in the presence of an enterprising opponent. Lee's attitude after the battle savors far more of bravado than a desire to be attacked. To block his retreat it would have been necessary to seize the Monterey Pass immediately after the battle.[3] Meade had the shorter line. His cavalry would have kept Lee at bay until the infantry could come up. He should never have suffered Lee to put

Lee in a Tight Place.

South Mountain between them without making an energetic effort to prevent it. As the Union army remained immovable until this was done, we have only to chronicle in brief the inglorious ending of an otherwise glorious campaign.

All the 4th the two armies lay in the positions just now described. Lee's direct line of retreat to the Potomac was by the Fairfield and Hagerstown road, which crossed the mountain below Read over and behind him through the Monterey Chap. I. defile. To withdraw his army and trains by this one road was altogether impracticable. The trains and wounded were therefore started off during the afternoon of the 4th, in a drenching rain, by the Chambersburg road, under a strong escort of cavalry and artillery, but no infantry.[4] When stretched out on the road this train was seventeen miles long.

Being ordered to push on to the Potomac without halting, the sufferings of the wounded were horrible beyond description. Travelling all night Lee's and avoiding Chambersburg, this col-Wounded. umn struck across the country to Greencastle, and after fighting its way all day against detachments of Union cavalry, finally got to the Potomac at Williamsport, on the afternoon of the 5th, with the loss of a few wagons. After the escort had passed through Greencastle, the citizens turned out and attacked the wagons in the rear with axes, so disabling some and delaying the rest.

When the wagon train got there, the Potomac was found too high to be forded. The bridges were gone, and the trains could not get across that way.[5] So there Lee met his first check.

After giving his trains a twelve hours' start, Lee put his army in motion for the Potomac by way of Fairfield and Hagerstown, by daylight of the 5th.

The road being unencumbered by trains,[6] the Confederates were able to move with celerity and silence. As soon as his departure was discovered, the Fifth and Sixth Corps moved out in pursuit. But it was then too late.

Lee's Infantry move off.

Lee had stolen a march on his pursuers. An officer of this force says of its tardy operations:—

"As we moved, a small rear-guard of the enemy

retreated. We followed it up to Fairfield, in a gorge of the mountains. There we again waited

A Lame Pursuit.

for them to go on. Then only one brigade, with the cavalry, continued to follow them, while the rest of the corps turned off to the left, toward Boonsboro," to which point the main body was now directing its march. Lee had got the short road and left Meade the long one.

Lee's army was thus safe back again in the Cumberland Valley before Meade was ready to pursue.[7] Having abandoned the idea of forcing the Monterey Pass, and so following up and

Union Army en Route.

harassing the enemy's rear, we have just seen the infantry turning off to the south, on the Gettysburg side of South Mountain, as if to head off Lee from the Potomac by this roundabout way, or, in short, by a march of fifty miles to his thirty, and after giving him a start of ten. This was to force the Union army to efforts which had just proved so exhausting. Nothing could exceed the impotence of this pursuit. In reality, the march up to Gettysburg to find and attack Lee was now being repeated. But fate, not Meade, was so checking Lee at every point that but for the weakness or delays of his adversary the Confederate general could never have saved his army as he did.

Even before Lee could reach Fairfield, General French[8] had reoccupied Harper's Ferry, destroyed the enemy's pontoon train at Williamsport and Falling Waters, and captured the guards. Finding his means of crossing gone, nothing remained for Lee but to show a bold front until they could be restored. And the long détour the Union army was making left him ample time in which to render his new position between Hagerstown and Williamsport so strong that when Meade[9] finally got his army up before it he again hesitated to attack. The tables were now fairly turned on him. His generals mostly shared in this feeling of respectful fear. Stung by the President's censure, Meade at last bestirred himself. Again he was too late. How often during this campaign have we been obliged to repeat those ill-omened words! In the language of the general-in-chief, Halleck:—

"Instead of attacking Lee in this position, with

Lee brought to a Halt.

the swollen waters of the Potomac in his rear, without any means of crossing his artillery, and when a defeat must have caused the surrender of his entire army, he was allowed time to construct a pontoon bridge with lumber collected from canal-boats and the ruins of wooden houses, and on the morning of the 1th his army had crossed to the south side of the river. His rear-guard, however, was attacked by our cavalry and suffered considerable loss. Thus ended the rebel campaign north of the Potomac, from which important political and military results had been expected. Our own loss in this short campaign had been very severe; namely, 2,834 killed, 13,709 wounded, and 6,643 missing—in all 23,182. We captured 3 guns, 41 tandards, 13,621 prisoners, 28, 178 small-arms."

Lee Escapes.

The Confederate losses, considering that they were always the assailants, must have exceeded these figures.[10] As it is well known that Pickett's losses were suppressed by Lee's order, any compilation must be necessarily incomplete.

Ten whole days thus elapsed from the time Lee fell back defeated from Cemetery Ridge until he recrossed the Potomac. He had brought off his army, his plunder, with upward of four thousand Union prisoners, by his opponent's leave, as one might say. There is a saying that a British army may be gleaned in a retreat, but not reaped. So far, in this war, barren victories had been the rule, and fruitful ones the rare exception.

We do not find much to say in praise of a retreat that was nowhere seriously molested. It has, we know, been lauded as a marvel of skill. Lee's patience alone was severely tested. The crossing of the Potomac was effected without hinderance in the presence of Meade's whole army, partly by the bridge at Falling Waters, partly by the fords at Williamsport. True, the Union cavalry did a great deal of hard riding and scouting; but it, too, failed to destroy Lee's trains on the 6th, when it was in its power to have done so, and, in all probability, compelled his surrender.

[1] Lee's cavalry had also left its menacing post in the Union rear.

[2] It has been claimed that the Union right was too much disordered for a counter-attack, and that one on the left was impracticable.

[3] Meade sent his cavalry out, not in a body, but in detachments, on the morning of the 4th. Gregg was ordered to the Chambersburg road, Kilpatrick to the Hagerstown, and Buford to Williamsport, by way

of Frederick. Kilpatrick attacked and dispersed the small force then guarding the Monterey Pass that evening, but no steps seem to have been taken for holding it, and Kilpatrick therefore went on over the mountains next day in pursuit of the enemy's trains. We observe, in this connection, that Lee threw every sabre he had into Meade's rear in anticipation of his retreat on July 3d.

4 Lee told the officer in command that he could spare him all the artillery he wanted, but no infantry.

5 The Union cavalry attacked this train on the 6th without success. Had they succeeded, all of Lee's immense plunder would have fallen into their hands. As it was, the trains were got across by a rope ferry; also the four thousand Union prisoners that the army brought along with it.

6 The corps trains had to move with the army mostly.

7 The whole Union army did not leave Gettysburg before the morning of the 6th. The Confederates were then nearly up to Hagerstown.

8 French, it will be remembered, had been ordered to hold Frederick. He now occupied the lower passes for which Meade was making, so reinforcing Meade.

9 The infantry reached Middletown on the morning of the 9th, crossed South Mountain that day, and on the next came in front of the enemy's intrenchments.

10 The Confederate losses have been variously estimated all the way from twenty thousand four hundred (total) to thirty thousand There exists no accurate basis for a fair count. The first figure is far too low; the last, perhaps, too high.

XI

THINGS BY THE WAY

THE battle of Gettysburg has often been called the turning-point of the war between the States. It was certainly the greatest of the many great conflicts of that war—the greatest exhibition, we will say, of stubborn fighting. There, if ever, it was that Greek met Greek. During three sweltering midsummer days, two numerous, well-appointed, veteran armies, ably led and equally nerved to their utmost efforts, fought for the mastery with equal resolution and bravery. For three days the result hung in suspense. Through all those terrible days the battle constantly grew in its proportions and intensity. From first to last, until the last gun was fired, the hush of expectancy fell upon the land. It was felt that this battle must be decisive. On one side, at least, was the determination to make it so. The impoverished Confederacy was staking its fortunes upon a last throw.

Yet this battle was singularly indecisive. On the first day the Union forces suffered a serious reverse; on the second they narrowly escaped a defeat; but on the third the Confederates were so signally repulsed that nothing was left them but retreat. This they effected with boldness and skill, in spite of the victors, in spite of the elements—in fine, in spite of that fortune which seemed to have turned against them from the moment of their defeat.

Considered, then, only as a battle, Gettysburg was a series of isolated combats, delivered without unity and followed by no irremediable reverse to the vanquished. In no military sense, therefore, can it be called decisive. In a political sense it was even less so, because Lee's army was neither destroyed, nor were the resources of the Confederacy fatally crippled. Rather was it a trial of strength between two athletes, one of whom, after throwing the other, tells him to get up and go about his business—in short, a mere pounding match.

Yet Gettysburg ought to have been the Waterloo of the Confederacy. Then and there that
war should have ended. To say that the whole
country was aghast at Lee's escape would be only
the plainest expression of the popular feeling of
the day. Naturally enough one great chorus of
disappointment greeted its announcement. Was
this all? Had these two armies merely had a
wrestling match? Had Meade and Lee compared
their bruises, only to separate with the understanding that they would fight again at some
future day when both felt stronger? Appar-
ently the war was no nearer its ending than
before. To the common understanding it did
seem "a most lame and impotent conclusion."
If the Confederates could not be crushed when
everything conspired against them, and in favor
of the Union army, when would they be?

That Lee extricated his army from its highly
dangerous position must no longer be attributed
to his superior generalship, we think, but to the
want of it on the Union side. It is vain to ask
why this or that thing was not done, since this
campaign is unique for its omissions. Meade at

Gettysburg was like a man who has been pushed into a fight reluctantly, and who stops the moment his adversary is down.

The history of this battle is largely that of the two commanders and their subordinates. Things done or left undone control the destinies of nations as well as of individuals. The want of cordiality among some of the Union generals was an incident of importance.

In arresting Lee's triumphal march, Meade had undoubtedly achieved all that the best-informed persons would have asked of him when he took the command, more perhaps than he allowed himself to expect when the magnitude of the task first unfolded itself to his troubled vision. His measures are so expressive of this want of confidence that any other conclusion seems inadmissible. Very sanguine persons, indeed, said that Lee ought never to return to Virginia except as a prisoner of war. The bare notion of a successful invasion by seventy thousand or eighty thousand men, with one hundred thousand behind them and the whole North before them, was scouted as a piece of folly designed and put in execution by madmen. If one hundred thousand were not enough, were there not one hundred and fifty thousand available? When Lee got to the Susquehanna these demands were somewhat lowered. They did not know, these unreflecting persons, that what an army wants is not men, but a man —one man.

So far this army had been a school in which mediocrity had risen. The really great commander had not yet forced his way to the front in spite of cabals in or out of the army. There had been a series of experiments—disastrous experiments. No army had ever marched more bravely to defeat or so seldom to victory. Few expected victory now.

Yielding to an imperative order, Meade found the Herculean task thrust upon him, with the fact staring him in the face that a defeated general meant a disgraced one.

But even then he did not find himself free to handle his army as he thought proper, because in Halleck he had always a tutor and critic who from his easy-chair in Washington assumed to supervise the acts of the commander in the field.

Upon a not over-confident general the effect was especially pernicious. The war-cry at Washington was, "Beat the enemy, but make no mistakes!" This was constantly ringing in Meade's ears. As Halleck was an excellent closet strategist, some of his suggestions would have been eminently proper and useful, could he have been on the spot himself, but under existing conditions they could serve only to make Meade still more hesitating and timid. Handled in this way, no army has ever achieved great results, and no army ever will achieve them.

At the close of the Third Day's sanguinary encounter with Lee, Meade had found himself victorious. The fact that the fortune of war had thus placed the initiative in his hands seems to have become a source of embarrassment and perplexity; from that moment his acts became timid, halting, partial. When pressed to more active measures he flew into a passion.

The fault, as we look at it, was not so much in the commander as in the man. Meade the commander could do no more than Meade the man. He was no genius. He was only a brave, methodical, and conscientious soldier, who, within his limitations, had acted well his part. Under Grant he made an excellent so-called second in command.

It has been said that in defending itself successfully, the Union army had done all that could be expected, under the circumstances. Must we then admit that for Lee not to conquer was in itself a victory? Unquestionably there was a prevalent, a somewhat overshadowing, feeling that all the best generalship was on the Confederate side.

By a sort of perversity of the human mind, a certain class of critics is always found ready to prove why a beaten general is the best general.

Nevertheless, Lee himself goes down in history as a general who never won a decisive victory.

He was certainly lucky at Gettysburg. For a time his great reputation silenced the voice of criticism. His own subordinates are now accusing him of making fatal mistakes. May it not be equally true that Lee rashly undertook more at Gettysburg than he was able to perform? He has as good as admitted it. Carried away by a first success, he committed the old mistake of underrating his adversary. His victory of the first day

was due to no combinations of his own, because
he was then completely ignorant of where the
Federal army was. He supposed it at least twenty
miles off. His success of the second, again, arose
first out of an entire misconception on his part
as to the Union position, which was nowhere near
where he thought it was, and next from a piece of
recklessness on the part of one of the Union generals, by which an inferior force was again opposed
to a superior one. On the third, he used means
wholly inadequate to the work in hand, yet of his
own planning; and on all three days, with the
field of battle under his eye, little or no manœu-
vring for advantage of position, and plenty of time
to look about him in, he signally failed to secure
coöperation among his corps commanders. We
see no evidence here, we confess, of generalship.
Indeed, this inability to make himself obeyed indicates a serious defect somewhere. Like another
great but also unfortunate captain, Lee might have
exclaimed in bitterness of spirit, "Incomprehen-
sible day! Concurrence of unheard-of fatalities!
Strange campaign when, in less than a week, I
three times saw assured victory escape from my

grasp! And yet all that skill could do was done."

Gettysburg made no reputations on either side. It may have destroyed some illusions in regard to the invincibility of Confederate generals. Meade succeeded because he was able to move troops to threatened points more rapidly than his assailant, but the battle was won more through the gallantry of the soldiers than by the skill of their generals. Victory restored to them their feeling of equality —their morale. And that was no small thing.

Considered with reference to its political effect upon the fortunes of the Confederacy, not to have succeeded was even worse than not to have tried at all, since it settled the question, once and for all, of achieving independence on Northern soil. Peace without submission was no longer possible, because the end was no longer in doubt. It came at last. And never in the history of the world, it is believed, have the victors shown such magnanimity to the vanquished.

THE END.

APPENDIX

ARMY OF THE POTOMAC AS IT FOUGHT AT GETTYSBURG.

Major-Gen. GEORGE G. MEADE, Commanding.

STAFF.

Major-Gen. Daniel Butterfield, Chief of Staff; Brig.-Gen. M. R. Patrick, Provost Marshal-General; Brig.-Gen. Seth Williams, Adjutant-General; Brig.-Gen. Edmund Shriver, Inspector-General; Brig.-Gen. Rufus Ingalls, Q. M. General; Brig.-Gen. Gouverneur K. Warren, Chief of Engineers; Brig.-Gen. Henry J. Hunt, Chief of Artillery; Col. Henry F. Clarke, Chief Commissary; Major John Letterman, Chief of Medical Department; Major D. W. Flagler, Chief Ordnance Officer; Capt. L. B. Norton, Chief Signal Officer.

FIRST ARMY CORPS.

Major-Gen. JOHN F. REYNOLDS.

First Division.—Brig.-Gen. James S. Wadsworth. *First Brigade:* Brig.-Gen. Solomon Meredith; *Second Brigade:* Brig.-Gen. Lysander Cutler. *Second Division.*—Brig.-Gen. John C. Robinson. *First Brigade:* Brig.-Gen. Gabriel R. Paul; *Second Brigade:* Brig.-Gen. Henry Baxter. *Third Division.*—Maj.-Gen. Abner Doubleday. *First Brigade:* Brig.-Gen. Thos. A. Rowley; *Second Brigade:* Col. Roy Stone; *Third Brigade:* Brig.-Gen. Geo. J. Stannard; *Artillery Brigade:* Col. Chas. S. Wainwright.

SECOND ARMY CORPS.

Major-Gen. WINFIELD S. HANCOCK.

First Division.—Brig.-Gen. John C. Caldwell. *First Brigade:* Col. Edwin E. Cross; *Second Brigade:* Col. Patrick Kelly; *Third Brigade:* Brig.-Gen. S. K. Zook; *Fourth Brigade:* Col. John R. Brooke. *Second Division.*—Brig.-Gen. John Gibbon. *First Brigade:* Brig.-Gen. William Harrow; *Second Brigade:* Brig.-Gen. Alex. S. Webb; *Third Brigade:* Col. Norman J. Hall.

APPENDIX 171

Third Division.—Brig.-Gen. Alexander Hays. *First Brigade:* Col. Samuel S. Carroll; *Second Brigade:* Col. Thomas A. Smyth; *Third Brigade:* Col. Geo. L. Willard; *Artillery Brigade:* Capt. J. G. Hazard.

Major-Gen. DANIEL E. SICKLES.

*First Division.—*Major-Gen. David B. Birney. *First Brigade:* Brig.-Gen. C. K. Graham; *Second Brigade:* Brig.-Gen. J. H. H. Ward; *Third Brigade:* Col. Philip R. De Trobriand.

*Second Division.—*Brig.-Gen. Andrew A. Humphreys. *First Brigade:* Brig.-Gen. Joseph B. Carr; *Second Brigade:* Col. Wm. R. Brewster; *Third Brigade:* Col. Geo. C. Burling; *Artillery Brigade:* Capt. Geo. E. Randolph.

Major-Gen. GEORGE B. SYKES.

*First Division.—*Brig.-Gen. James Barnes. *First Brigade:* Col. W. S. Tilton; *Second Brigade:* Col. J. B. Sweitzer; *Third Brigade:* Col. Strong Vincent.

APPENDIX

Second Division.—Brig.-Gen. Romayn B. Ayres. *First Brigade:* Col. Hannibal Day; *Second Brigade:* Col. Sidney Burbank; *Third Brigade:* Brig.-Gen. S. H. Webb.

*Third Division.—*Brig.-Gen. S. Wiley Crawford *First Brigade:* Col. Wm. McCandless; *Second Brigade:* Col. Joseph W. Fisher; *Artillery Brigade:* Capt. A. P. Martin.

Major-Gen. JOHN SEDGWICK.

*First Division.—*Brig.-Gen. H. G. Wright. *First Brigade:* Brig.-Gen. A. T. A. Torbert; *Second Brigade:* Brig.-Gen. J. J. Bartlett; *Third Brigade:* Brig.-Gen. D. A. Russell.

Second Division.—Brig.-Gen. A. P. Howe. *Second Brigade:* Col. L. A. Grant; *Third Brigade:* Brig.-Gen. T. H. Neill.

*Third Division.—*Brig.-Gen. Frank Wheaton. *First Brigade:* Brig.-Gen. Alex. Shaler; *Second Brigade:* Cal. H. L. Eustis; *Third Brigade:* Col. David J. Nevin; *Artillery Brigade:* Col. C. H. Tompkins

ELEVENTH ARMY CORPS.

Major-Gen. OLIVER O. HOWARD.

First Division.—Brig.-Gen. Francis C. Barlow. *First Brigade:* Col. Leopold von Gilsa; *Second Brigade:* Brig.-Gen. Adelbert Ames.

Second Division.—Brig.-Gen. A. von Steinwehr. *First Brigade:* Col. Chas. R. Coster; *Second Brigade:* Cal. Orlando Smith.

Third Division.—Major-Gen. Carl Shurz. *First Brigade:* Brig.-Gen. A. von Schimmelpfennig; *Second Brigade:* Col. Waldimir Kryzanowski; *Artillery Brigade:* Maj. Thos. W. Osborn.

TWELFTH ARMY CORPS.

Major-Gen. HENRY W. SLOCUM.

First Division.—Brig.-Gen. Alpheus S. Williams. *First Brigade:* Col. Archibald L. McDongall; *Second Brigade:* Brig.-Gen. Henry H. Lockwood; *Third Brigade:* Col. Silas Colgrove.

Second Division.—Brig.-Gen. John W. Geary. *First Brigade:* Col. Chas. Candy; *Second Brigade:* Col. Geo. A. Cobham, Jr.; *Third Brigade:* Brig.-Gen. Geo. S. Greene; *Artillery Brigade:* Lieut. Edw. D. Muhlenberg.

CAVALRY CORPS.

Major-Gen. ALFRED PLEASONTON.

First Division.—Brig.-Gen. John Buford. *First Brigade:* Col. Wm. Gamble; *Second Brigade:* Col. Thos. C. Devin; *Reserve Brigade:* Brig.-Gen. Wesley Merritt.

Second Division.—Brig.-Gen. D. McM. Gregg. *First Brigade:* Col. J. B. McIntosh; *Second Brigade:* Col. Pennock Huey; *Third Brigade:* Col. J. I. Gregg.

Third Division.—Brig.-Gen. Judson Kilpatrick. *First Brigade:* Brig.-Gen. Elon J. Farnsworth; *Second Brigade:* Brig.-Gen. Geo. A. Custer,

HORSE ARTILLERY.

First Brigade: Capt. John M. Robertson; *Second Brigde:* Capt. John C. Tidball.

ARTILLERY RESERVE.

Brig.-Gen. R. O. TYLER.

First Regular Brigade: Capt. D. R. Ransom; *First Volunteer Brigade:* Lieut.-Col. F. McGilvery; *Second Volunteer Brigade:* Capt. E. D. Taft; *Third Volunteer Brigade:* Capt. James F. Huntington; *Fourth Volunteer Brigade:* Capt. R. H. Fitzhugh.

INDEX

ARMY OF THE POTOMA follows Lee, 39; order of march, 40; halts at Frederick, Md., 40; change of commanders, 40; dangerous meddling, 41; effect on the army, 42; its *morale*, 43, 44; its efficiency, *note*, 45; in march toward the enemy, 49; diverging while the enemy is concentrating, 52; hard marching, 53; is badly scattered, 53; left wing in a critical position, 54; how posted on June 30, 55; Buford's cavalry engaged at Gettysburg, 62; First Corps gets up to its support, 63: holds the ground till the Eleventh arrives, 68; both are defeated, 76; losses, 77; reasons for defeat, 77; ordered to Gettysburg, 85; Twelfth Corps gets up, 87; also part of Third, 89; other corps, 90; strength of the corps, *note*, 96; as posted July 2 on Cemetery Ridge, 98; Third Corps movements, 101, *et seq.;* how this corps was formed to resist Lee's attack, 109; whole of the army up at last, 109; the battle begins, 112; Sickles' whole line is driven in, 124; we hold Little Round Top, 121; portions of the Second and Fifth assist the Third; they have to fall back, 123; other troops compel Longstreet to desist, 125; dispositions for renewing the battle, 133, 134; Culp's Hill attacked, 135; EWEll

driven out, 136; sustains a terrific cannonade, 137, 138, 139; lines as formed to resist charge of July 3, 140; the assault repulsed, 143, *et Seq.;* remains inactive, 153; while Lee retreats, 154; marches in pursuit, 154; finds enemy in a strong position, 156; *notes,* 159; and Lee again slips away, 157; losses during the campaign, 157.

BALTIMORE alarmed, *note,* 45.
Baltimore Pike, cutting the Union lines, 99.
Battlefield Memorial Association, *note,* 21.
Buford's (John) cavalry operations on the left, 40; riding to Fairfield, 49; finds the enemy, 54; is ordered to hold Gettysburg, 55; posts himself on Oak Ridge, 61; fights till relieved, 63; is sent off to the rear, 101.

CAVALRY, battles of July 3d, 148; operations during Lee's retreat, *notes,* 158.
Carlisle, Pa., occupied, 29; evacuated, 51.
Cemetery Ridge, described, 15,16; becomes a rallying-point, July 1, 77; situation afternoon of July 1, 82; Hancock renders it secure, 87; described more in detail, 98, *et seq.;* the enemy succeed in scaling it, July 2, 125, 128; but are repulsed, 129; its ad-

176 INDEX

vantages for defence better availed of, 130.

Chambersburg, Pa., occupied by Lee's cavalry, 25; becomes his headquarters, 27.

Confederate Army, The, eludes ours, *note*, 32; and invades Pennsylvania, 23; its strength, 24; its composition, *note*, 32; points of superiority, 24, 25; its *personnel*, 26, 27; at Chambersburg, 26, 27; moves to York and Carlisle, 28; its spirit, 29; moves to concentrate, 52; its advance upon Gettysburg is disputed, 62; finally defeats the forces opposed to it, 69, *et seq.;* losses, *note,* 80; all but one division up night of July 1, 91; how formed, *note,* 110; the attack on Sickles, 115; Sickles defeated, 123; Longstreet's losses, 125; Cemetery Ridge reached by Hill's troops, 125; Ewell gains a foothold at Culp's Hill, 126; advantage to the Confederates, 127; position at close of the day, *note,* 131; Ewell expelled from Culp's Hill, 136; cannonades Union position, 137; final attack repulsed, 141, *et seq.;* evacuates Gettysburg, 150; getting ready to retreat, 150; retreat effected, 157; losses, *note,* 159.

Culp's Hill, its relation to Cemetery Hill, 19; occupied by Union troops, 84; made secure, 87; enemy gain a lodgment at, 126; retaken, 136.

Cumberland Valley, route of Lee's invasion, 23; exodus from, 34.

Curtin, A. G., his efforts to meet the invasion, 36.

Devil's Den, The, situation of, 20; surroundings, *note,* 22; struggle for its possession, 115, 116, 117; in the enemy's hands, *note,* 131.

Early's (J. E.) operations around York, 28; as a blind, *note,* 33; recalled to Gettysburg, 52; his arrival decides the day, 73, 76; assaults Cemetery Hill, July 2, 128; but is forced out, 129.

Emmettsburg Road, described, 21; picketed by Union troops. 88: its relation 'to the hostile armies; 99; becomes a point of direction for Longstreet's attack, 114.

Ewell's Confederate corps at Chambersburg, 26; moves on to Carlisle and York, 28; moves to Gettysburg and decides the first of July, 69, *et seq.;* but hesitates to attack Cemetery Hill, 81.

Frederick, Md., becomes the pivot for the Union army, 40.

Gettysburg, described, 10, 11; its strategic value, 13, 14, 15, *et seq.;* its topography, 15, 16, *et seq.;* Cemetery Ridge, 16; Seminary Ridge, 17; commanding points, 19, 20; Cemetery Ridge as a defensive line, 20; *notes* 1, 2, and 3, p. 21; memorials of battle, *note,* 21; first appearance of Confederates in, 28; and *note,* 33; Lee's whole army marching to, 52; Union forces approaching, 55; how and where the battle began, see Chap. V., p. 60; in first day's conflict, 60, *et seq.;* occupied by Ewell, 78; evacuated, 150.

Great Round Top, how situated, 19.

Hancock, Winfield S., organizing victory from defeat, 81, 82, 83; orders Culp's Hill occupied, 84; his report to Meade, 85; *note,* 95; sends Geary's division to Little Round Top, 88.

Harrisburg alarmed, 25; enemy near it, 29; the panic at, 34, *et seq.;* militia ordered to, 37; narrow escape of, 50.

Heth's (Harry) Confederate division approaches Gettysburg first, 52; encounters Buford's cavalry, 62; brings on battle of July 1, 63; sustains a check, 66; Pender, Rodes, and Early come to his aid, 69, 75; takes part in the famous charge of July 3, 140, 141.

Hood, John B., marches into Chambersburg, 26, 27; attacks the Union left, July 2d, 114; is wounded, 115; his attack checked, 117; Union cavalry in his rear, 148.

Hooker's (Joseph) plan of campaign, 40; objections to, *note,* 45; is superseded, 40.

Howard, Oliver O., takes command at Gettysburg, 70; calls in vain for help, 70, 71.

L e e, Robert E., his ascendancy over his troops, 29; portrait of, 30; wants his cavalry badly, 38; feels what it is to be in an enemy's country, 39; plans thwarted by Meade, 50; decides to cross South Mountain and give battle, 50; *note,* 59; orders all corps to Gettysburg, 51; steals a march on Meade, 53; at Gettysburg, 81; decides to attack, 91; Longstreet to turn Union left, 94; the plan in detail, 105, 106; determines to renew the battle, 133; reinforces Ewell, 133; orders Longstreet to assault Cemetery Ridge, 134; sends off his wounded, 153; follows with his army, 154; gets to the Potomac before he can be intercepted, 156; and crosses to Virginia safely, 157.

Little Round Top, its position

and appearance, 19; *note,* 22; Hancock causes its occupation, 88; is abandoned, 98; is about to fall into the enemy's hands, 115; troops brought up to it, 119, 120; conflict for its possession, 120, 121; Union troops remain masters, 121.

Longstreet, James, opposes Lee's purpose, 91; is ordered to begin the attack of July 2, 105; gets into position, 106; as a fighter, 106, 107; method of attacking Sickles, 114, 115; is successful here, but halts before the main position, 125.

Lutheran Church a hospital, 22.

Lutheran Seminary, its situation, 17; Union troops make a stand there, 77.

M cLaws, (Lafayette) Confederate division attacks Sickles, July 2, 117.

Meade, George G., takes command, 42; his qualifications, 43; divining Lee's intentions, 47, 48; discards Hooker's plan, 48; his own, 49; transfers his base to Westminster, 49; relieves Harrisburg and York, 51; his perplexities, 51; is outmanœuvred, 53; learns that Lee is moving to the east of South Mountain, 55; but holds his purpose of concentrating at Big Pipe Creek, 57; learns of the defeat at Gettysburg and sends Hancock there with full powers, 70; decides to fight at Gettysburg, 85; though the chances are against him, 90; gets to the field, 94; designs attacking Lee himself, 97; posting his troops, 98; depressed by the results of July 2 he calls a council of war which decides to fight it out, 132; sends troops to retake Culp's Hill, 133; starts his cavalry on

INDEX

Printed in the United States
66820LVS00002B/13-18